OVERSIZE

AN INTRODUCTION TO

GREEK MYTHOLOGY

AN INTRODUCTION TO

GREEK
MYTHOLOGY

DAVID BELLINGHAM

Grange
BOOKS

A QUANTUM BOOK

Published by Grange Books
an imprint of Grange Books Plc
The Grange
Kingsnorth Industrial Estate
Hoo, nr. Rochester
Kent ME3 9ND

Copyright ©1989 Quintet Publishing Limited

This edition printed 1998

ISBN 1-85627-957-X

QUMGRM

This book is produced by
Quantum Books Ltd
6 Blundell Street
London N7 9BH

Printed in Singapore by Star Standard Industries Pte. Ltd

Contents

Introduction

Our word 'myth' derives from the ancient Greek word *muthos* which originally meant 'utterance' and came to mean 'a spoken or written story'. The Greek word *muthologia* meant 'talking about, or retelling stories'. Today, 'mythology' refers both to the body of myths of a society and to the study of those myths. There is, however, no precise definition of the word myth and scholars tend to divide myths into three main types: legends, folktales and 'pure' myths.

LEGENDS The importance of mythology to the ancient Greeks can be gauged by the subjects of their earliest surviving poems. In the 8th century BC, the poet Homer produced the first written version of the legends surrounding the Greek siege of Troy; these have survived as the epic poems the *Iliad* and the *Odyssey*. Legends deal with real events and people, but contain unreal elements normally associated with myth: meetings between mortals and gods, super-human feats, magic and monsters. There are several possible reasons for this mixture of the real and the fantastic. The actual events of the Trojan War occurred some four centuries before Homer, at a time when the Greek world was run by kings who lived in luxurious palaces defended by high stone walls. Though these royal communities were relatively civilized, there was no written literature; therefore the history of events such as the Trojan War had to be passed down from generation to generation by poets relying on memory. This early poetry was designed to entertain and instruct the members of the royal courts, who identified with the heroes of the stories – after all, these heroes were their ancestors. Therefore, it is hardly surprising to find the poets glamourizing the Greek heroes as well as embroidering the facts with mythical stories of gods and monsters.

'PURE' MYTHS Hesiod, a contemporary of Homer, wrote the *Theogony* in which the Greek account of the creation of the world and its giants, gods and mortals was recorded for the first time. Again, there must have been many different versions of the story, passed down through the preceding centuries by the oral poets. Although Hesiod's poem is basically a catalogue of the divine family tree, the poet occasionally breaks the monotony by relating a self-contained 'pure' myth – that is, a myth relating directly to religion and ritual. For example, Hesiod's myth of Prometheus defined the early relationship between man and gods and 'explained' the nature of the animal sacrifices in Greek religious rituals. Likewise, Hesiod's myth of the 'Ages of Man' sought to explain why the Greek world of the 8th century BC was a violent and greedy place. There had once been a 'Golden Age' in which mortals and gods lived happily together on earth; Mother

BELOW *View of Mycenae: the Classical Greeks romanticized their prehistoric Mycenaean ancestors, believing that the huge stone walls had been built by the giant Cyclopes race: we still call this architectural style 'Cyclopean'. Traditionally the palace of King Agamemnon, who led the Greek army against Troy.*

Earth produced everything for man's consumption and manual labour was unnecessary. Unfortunately, the men became inquisitive and began to sail their ships to foreign lands from which they would return laden with riches; this newly acquired wealth had to be defended and the first city walls were built. Mother Earth was shut outside and men had to extract her natural gifts by force, using the same iron for their ploughs which they had used for their weapons. With the advent of greed and war the gods departed to the heavens in disgust. According to Hesiod, Greek culture had regressed from the Age of Gold, through the Silver and Bronze and Heroic Ages to his own Iron Age. However, there was an educational motive for this myth: Hesiod pleaded with his royal audience to refrain from greed and violence so that the Golden Age might return, a plea that was repeated by later poets.

FOLKTALES As the name suggests, folktales were mythical stories intended for the uneducated farming communities outside the palaces and cities. The heroes of folktales were often ordinary men and women as opposed to the royal princes and princesses of the poetic myths. Generally the social purpose of folktales was moral and cautionary rather than religious and ritualistic. Myths tended to come in the form of highly sophisticated poetry, whereas folktales were told as straightforward prose narratives or simple poems.

It is impossible to say whether all Greeks actually believed in their myths. By the Classical period (5th century BC) the Greek city-states had become complex social structures; wealthy citizens were educated in a wide range of subjects and although they read mythical and legendary poetry, they also studied philosophy which had developed rational explanations for most natural phenomena. Therefore myths might no longer have

been seen as 'true stories' in sophisticated circles, but they continued to be referred to in every type of writing.

Our knowledge of Greek myths derives mainly from their literature, but it is rare to find a complete myth contained in a single piece of literature. As already referred to in the case of Homer and Hesiod, writing had developed relatively late in Greece, by which time the myths and legends were widely known from the oral tradition. Later writers could therefore depend on this knowledge in their audience, and concentrate on certain undeveloped aspects of the earlier stories. The consequent fragmentation of the surviving myths was accelerated by later poets who tended to alter them, giving different endings or explanations for a character's behaviour. These changes were not for variety only, but often reflected contemporary social attitudes. The female poet Sappho defended the behaviour of Helen of Troy as being divinely inspired, whilst male writers tended to blame the Trojan war on what they saw to be either feminine weakness or whorish behaviour. Likewise the writers of tragedies used the mythical framework of their plays to air the political and social problems of the day: thus legendary kings were often represented as contemporary tyrants threatening the new democracy of Classical Athens.

The Greek poet would use the myth as an entertaining story that would retain the audience's attention while allowing the poet to make contemporary implications. Theseus was seen in the 5th century BC as the hero of the new Athenian democracy and artists depicted him defeating uncivilized giants and Centaurs, symbols of the barbarian Persians who had invaded Greece earlier in the century.

Greek mythology bears many similarities to other ancient mythologies. This is particularly evident in the relationship of gods and heroes. In Norse mythology the god Odin can be compared to the Greek Zeus: Zeus ruled in Olympus, Odin in Valhalla;

ABOVE *View of the countryside at the monastery of Osios Loukas near Athens. The landscape, with its olive groves and wild limestone hills, has hardly changed since Classical times.*

ABOVE Charon on the River Styx; *Athenian white-ground* lekythos *(funerary oil container), late 5th century BC. Terracotta vases are a visually important source of our knowledge of the Greek myths and the subjects usually reflect their function: Charon is apt for a vase used in burial rituals.*

both used thunderbolts as weapons and both had angry wives, Hera and Frigg, ever-jealous of their affairs with mortal women; each had a favourite warrior daughter, Athene and Brunhild. The three Moerae (Fates) of Greek mythology sat and span mortal destinies; the Norns did the same in Norse mythology. The Norse heroes performed similar super-human exploits. Thus Siegfried slew the dragon Fafnir and fell in love with the divine Brunhild.

Since the 19th century this comparative mythology has become a serious academic discipline and many other links have been discovered between the myths of cultures as far apart as India and Celtic Britain. The Greek hero Heracles has been compared to both the Indian Sisupala and the Germanic Starkadr: for example, each hero was born with too much strength, had a divine helper and a divine enemy, and became immortal by a suicide brought about by a mortal assistant whom they rewarded with a supernatural gift: thus, in some traditions, Heracles gave his magic bow to Philoctetes who lit the hero's pyre. So striking are the similarities that scholars have used the comparison as evidence for a common 'Indo-European' cultural heritage.

In the 20th century we have created our own myths. Popular comic-strip heroes such as Superman and Wonderwoman often reflect the ancient Greek heroes. Wonderwoman was actually born from Greek myth as Diana, daughter of Hippolyte, Queen of the Amazons. Her creator, Charles Moulton, introduced her in 1941: 'At last, in a world torn by the hatreds and wars of men, appears a woman to whom the problems and feats of men are mere childsplay. With a hundred times the agility and strength of our best male athletes and strongest wrestlers, she appears as though from nowhere to avenge an injustice or right a wrong. As lovely as Aphrodite, as wise as Athena, with the speed of Mercury and the strength of Hercules, she is known only as *Wonderwoman!*'.

Modern heroes, like their ancient counterparts, exhibit extraordinary physical powers. The Greek Achilles was invulnerable except on his heel and Superman could only be destroyed by green Kryptonite: these weak points enable ordinary mortals to identify with the heroes. The heroes also tend to fall in love with someone they save: thus the Greek Perseus married Princess Andromeda after rescuing her from the sea-monster; Wonderwoman likewise fell in love with the airline pilot whom she had rescued after a crash.

The Greeks sometimes turned living men into heroes. Alexander the Great died in 323 BC; he was only 33 years old, but had built an empire from India to Egypt. In imitation of the mythical heroes such as Heracles, he argued that his father was Zeus and proceeded to 'prove' his divine parentage to the rest of the world by means of his heroic military campaigns. After his tragic early death his life-story was mythologized and the more youthful Greek and Roman military leaders regarded him as their hero, to the extent of even copying his famous hairstyle in their portraits. We have similar 20th-century 'living legends' whom we have likewise transformed into mythical figures by confusing their glamourized and hyped media images with reality.

In this book many of the myths have been grouped according to types of subject, such as heroic tales and tragic romances: this will enable the reader to appreciate the different kinds of story that interested the Greeks, but it will be noticed that many of the individual stories contain a mixture of legend, folktale and 'pure' myth. I have used the traditional Romanized spellings of names, but have retained the Greek forms of names like Heracles and Hermes (not the Roman Hercules or Mercury – see the Appendix for a list of comparative Greek and Roman name forms).

Finally, for the sake of narrative flow, I have selected my own favourite versions of the myths and only occasionally refer to alternate versions.

ABOVE The introduction of Heracles to Olympus by Hermes and Athene; *Athenian black-figure* lekythos *(funerary oil container), 6th century* BC. *The deification of the mortal hero was an appropriate subject for this vase destined for an Athenian grave.*

ABOVE *Silver coin showing Alexander the Great and Zeus, and a marble copy of the original portrait head by the sculptor Lysippos. On the coin, Alexander wears Heracles' lion-skin, raising him to superhuman levels. The reverse depicts Zeus with his eagle – Alexander, like Heracles, claimed Zeus to be his real father. Alexander controlled his image by allowing only one sculptor (Lysippos) and one painter (Apelles) to portray him. The dramatic deep-set eyes, rather anxious heavy forehead and windswept hair, parted off-centre, were immediately recognizable in antiquity; these features were repeated in images of later generals who wished to emulate Alexander's heroism.*

The Birth of the Gods

The earliest and also the fullest account of the creation and the birth of the giants and gods is to be found in Hesiod's poem, the 'Theogony' (literally, 'The Birth of the Gods'). Hesiod lived in the 8th century BC at the time when the Greeks first introduced writing skills. We must assume that his account is the culmination of centuries of poems told from memory and handed from generation to generation in an oral tradition. As with other Greek myths, it cannot therefore be considered the only version of the story, but Hesiod's was the most influential source for later poets. There are remarkable parallels with the creation myths of the Hittites and Babylonians, whose literary versions were produced five centuries earlier. Recent archaeological and literary studies have suggested a much greater level of contact between Greece and the Orient than was previously thought for this early period, and Hesiod is now considered to have produced a mixture of oriental and Greek mythology. There was no single divine creator in Greek mythology; the Earth and the Sky 'emerged' from the void and together gave birth to worldly life forms.

First there was Chaos, a chasm without shape or light. The ample-breasted Gaia (Mother Earth) emerged, where one day gods and men would dwell; deep beneath her swirled the mists of Tartarus, later the prison of rebellious giant Titans; and then appeared the most handsome god of all, Eros (Sexual Love), who numbs our limbs and defeats our reason – he has the same effect on the immortal gods. No birth of gods, giants, animals or men would have taken place without his power of attraction.

From the chasm came the two dark ones, Erebus (Dark Underworld) beneath Gaia and Nyx (Night) above her. Eros was present; Nyx and Erebus made love and Nyx gave birth to her brilliant and beautiful children; Aether (Upper Air) with his azure satin cloak stretched across the top of the sky; and his sister Hemera (Day) who steps out of Tartarus bringing us light and returns in the twilight, greeting her mother, Nyx, on the other side of the road.

THE BIRTH OF THE TITANS

Meanwhile lonely Gaia felt the touch of Eros and produced a lover of herself and for herself; his name was Uranus (Heaven) and he covered her with his black velvet cloak, decorated with glittering stars, amongst which the gods would later make a home. Gaia twisted and turned and formed Ourea (the mountains), the home of Oreads (mountain-nymphs); from her came also never-draining Pontus (sea).

Eros produced a longing in Gaia for her own son Uranus, who showered her with heavenly rain and produced the swirling depths of Oceanus, the river which encircles mother Gaia. Oceanus was the first of the Titans, children of Gaia and Uranus. Next came Thea and Phoebe and their famous sisters, Tethys of the sea, Themis and Rhea of the earth, and Mnemosyne (Memory) who helps us to recall our myths; their brothers were Coeus, Crius and Iapetus and dazzling Hyperion of the sun. But the youngest was wicked little Cronus, whose schemings would later dethrone lusty Uranus, the father he despised. Later still, the three Cyclopes were born. They had only one eye at the centre of their foreheads and were skilful and crafty smiths. Their names were Brontes (Thunder), Steropes (Lightning), and Arges (Whitebolt); it was they who later forged the mighty thunderbolt of Olympian Zeus. More children were born to Gaia and Uranus, each one more monstrous then the last: the three Hecatoncheires brothers – Cottus, Gyes and Obriareus – each with 100 hands and fifty heads. Their appearance was abhorrent to Uranus, who feared and loathed his own offspring. As they were born, he pushed them back into the cavernous recesses of Gaia's womb, and delighted in her painful groans.

Gaia in her despair made a huge scythe from grey adamant and, showing it to her imprisoned children, said, 'My dear ones, would you dare to put an end to your father's evil ways?'. Young Cronus replied, 'I am not afraid of my cruel father. It would be right to put an end to his unspeakable behaviour; after all, it is of his own doing.' Gaia explained her plot to Cronus, handed him the awesome sickle and took him to a shady place for the ambush.

At twilight lusty Uranus appeared, walking alongside Nyx, his aunt. In his usual violent manner he mounted Gaia, smothering her with his black bejewelled cloak. Immediately Cronus grabbed Uranus's genitals and, with one sweep of the sharp-toothed sickle, cut them off and threw them carelessly behind him. The drops of blood which bespattered Gaia produced the Erinyes (Furies), who in memory of their birth haunt those who murder their own kin. The genitals themselves landed on the beach. The waves caressed them in the presence of Eros and Himerus (Desire) and soon white foam appeared and a girl was born. She came ashore on Cythera, then appeared in Cyprus as a beautiful goddess, and, because she was born from the foam, was named Aphrodite (literally 'foam-born').

Uranus in his anger gave his children the unflattering name of Titans. We also call them Giants.

NYX AND HER CHILDREN

Meanwhile Nyx produced many children of her own. From her came many of the dark and gloomy forces which oppress us: she it was who gave us our Fate and our Death, our Sleep and Dreams, and Misery with whom no god will sleep. As a reason for the gods to despise us she produced Nemesis, the goddess of retribution, who inspires both the gods and mortals with feelings of resentment when our fellow men misbehave. Dreadful Nyx gave us the facts of life we curse: Old Age, Deceit and hard-hearted Eris (Strife), who in turn bore Battles and Slaughter, Pretence and Arguments between neighbours, and Oath who strikes when we swear a falsehood.

BELOW *Sandro Botticelli (1444–1510)*, The Birth of Venus. *Using ancient literary descriptions Botticelli 'recreated' lost easel-paintings by famous Greek painters which would have pleased his classically educated patrons. In this painting Aphrodite appears in a well known Hellenistic pose which Botticelli adapted from an antique statue. The shell appeared in ancient versions of the birth.*

LEFT *Eustache Le Sueur (1616–55)*, The Sea Gods and the God of Love. *Two sailors (left) are approached by Poseidon with his trident, Tritons blowing conch shells, and Nereids. The presence of Cupids would suggest the impending mermaid-like 'marriage' of the doomed sailors to the Nereids.*

NEREUS

Pontus (Sea) produced with his mother Gaia the resplendent gods of the sea: from them came Nereus, the Old Man of the Sea, so kind and trustworthy and blessed with many lovely children – fifty girls who play in the watery lap of their grandfather Pontus. Such wonderful names they have: Speo the swift, rosy-armed Hipponoe, Galatea the beautiful, Amphitrite of the pretty ankles and Halimede with her gleaming diadem, floating beside Euarne with her perfect figure, a joy to behold.

Gaia lay with her son Nereus and bore huge Thaumas who married Electra, a daughter of deep Oceanus. Thaumus and Electra had peculiar children: Iris, a messenger of the gods, fleet of foot she is, and when she sometimes stops to catch her breath, we see a rainbow, carrying all the colours of heaven down to earth; how she raises our spirits after the storms created by angry Zeus! Yet the sisters of Iris are the Harpies, they look so pretty with their lovely hair, racing along in the storm-gales faster than birds, but many have they snatched from the earth as they fly, friends whom we never meet again.

THE CHILDREN OF CETO AND PHORCYS

The brother of Thaumas was noble Phorcys, who, admiring the splendid cheeks of his sister Ceto, lay with her to produce the Old Women, the Graeae; grey haired, they have only a single tooth and one eye between them, which they share. Ceto also bore the Gorgons; they live near Oceanus in the farthest regions of the earth, past the Atlas mountains, neighbours of Nyx and the sweet-singing Hesperides sisters, who guard the golden apples of the tree given by Gaia to Hera when she married Zeus. The Gorgon sisters are Stheno, Euryale and Medusa. Unlike her sisters, Medusa was mortal and one day when she was sitting in a meadow, surrounded by the first flowers of spring, the god with the sable locks,

LEFT The Gorgon Medusa; *painted terracotta plaque, 6th century* BC. *Such 'apotropaic' plaques decorated the roofs of Greek temples and were intended to frighten away evil spirits. The kneeling pose was used by Archaic Greek artists to suggest a running figure.*

Poseidon, made love to her; but she never saw her children for the hero Perseus cut off her head as a gift for a king. From her neck sprang Chrysaor with his golden sword, father of the three-headed giant Geryon whom Heracles killed for his cattle, and Pegasus, the wonderful winged horse.

As if that were not enough troublesome children for Ceto and Phorcys, one day a real monster was born to them, Echidna by name; the gods gave her a cave deep beneath the earth, because neither they nor mortal men could bear her, for although she looked quite normal from the waist up, her lower half was serpent, all snake-like and slippery.

THE CHILDREN OF ECHIDNA

Typhon, the Titan offspring of Gaia and Tartarus, became Echidna's friend and a number of fearsome offspring were produced, some of them now famous: Orthus the two-headed dog who helped to guard Geryon's cattle, but was killed by an arrow of Heracles; and the much more formidable guard-dog of Hades, Cerberus; some say he has as many as fifty heads and a resounding bark like a bronze cauldron struck by a sword. There was also the terrible Hydra of Lerna, object of one of Heracles' labours; you cut off one head and she grew two more. A worthy sister for the Hydra was the fire-breathing Chimaera; now she had just three heads, but one was a lion, one a goat, and one a snake. The hero Bellerophon would one day kill her, helped by his winged steed Pegasus. Echidna did not mind whether she loved Titan or monster, and even had children by her own son, the dog Orthus; to this couple were born the famous riddling Sphinx, who brought death to so many Thebans before Oedipus solved the problem, and the Nemean Lion,

whose pelt Heracles wore after slaying it for his first labour.

The last of Echidna's children was the serpent Ladon that guards the golden apples of the Hesperides.

THE CHILDREN OF TETHYS AND OCEANUS

Tethys, lovely daughter of Gaia and Uranus, lay with brother Oceanus and their children were the elegant-ankled Oceanids (sea-nymphs) and the river-gods of the earth – the Nile, the fair-flowing Danube, and those that run through Greece. The Oceanids were also joined by other beautiful nymphs, spirits of nature: the Naiads who swim in the rivers and springs; the Dryads who dwell in the trees; the Oreads of the mountains;

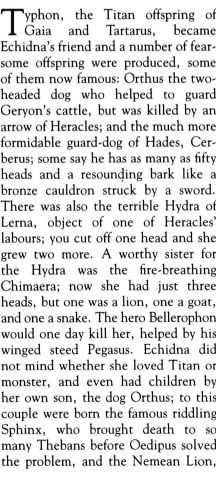

RIGHT Nereid riding the waves on a sea-bird; *late 5th century* BC. *She was one of several Nereids standing between the columns of a royal tomb at Xanthus in East Greece: in this funerary context the figures were probably symbolic of the journey to the after-life. The drapery is suitably wet and clinging.*

13

the Nereids of the sea. Lucky the man who glimpses them, for they bring good fortune to those who treat them with respect; but woe to that man who abuses them, who cuts a sacred tree or pollutes a spring.

THE CHILDREN OF THEA AND HYPERION

Thea and Hyperion, sister and brother of Tethys, also had children: the mighty Helius (the Sun) took after his father; by day he is woken by his rosy-fingered sister Eos (Dawn) and rides across the sky in a four-horse chariot, sinking into Oceanus at dusk to refresh his tired horses; at night he floats eastwards along Oceanus in a golden bowl. His shining sister Selene (the Moon) drives her chariot by night, a dimmer light so as not to wake us.

THE CHILDREN OF EOS AND ASTRAEUS

Astraeus was born to two other children of Gaia, Crius and Eurybia. Mist-born Eos and starry Astraeus gave birth to the bright Morning Star and many other shining ones in the garland of heaven; to them were born also the flint-hearted Winds: Zephyrus comes with his clearing breezes from the west; Boreas rushes down from the north; Notus comes up from the south and Argestes blows from the east.

THE CHILDREN OF STYX AND PALLAS

Pallas was a brother of Astraeus and together with the stream of Styx, an Oceanid, brought into the world Aspiration and winged Nike (Victory) with her trim ankles, and their outstanding brothers Power and Strength; all four never leave the side of thundering Zeus, they sit beside his throne and follow him wherever he goes. On that fateful day when Zeus summoned the immortal gods to Mount Olympus for a counsel of war against the Titans, he pledged, 'I shall give to any of you who fight alongside me all the privileges and honours which our cruel father Cronus denies you. This shall be our justice and revenge.' Oceanus sensibly sided with the Olympians and sent his ever-flowing daughter Styx to pledge the family's eternal loyalty. Zeus blessed her waters and made her a symbol of oaths taken by the gods and he took her children under his protection.

THE CHILDREN OF PHOEBE AND COEUS

The Titans Coeus and Phoebe were brother and sister of Cronus, and to these two were born Leto of the sable gown, loved by men and gods for her gentleness and as mother of the two Olympians, Apollo and Artemis. Her grand-daughter was Hecate, one of the few Titans not despised by Zeus, who made her the nurse of our young children; powerful Hecate moves between heaven, earth and sea, and brings success by standing beside all who worship her, be they fighters, farmers, athletes or fishermen.

THE CHILDREN OF RHEA AND CRONUS

At last some gods were born to Cronus and his sister Rhea: Hestia who protects the hearth of our houses; Demeter who dwells beneath the earth and sends up cereal crops through the soil; Hera of the golden sandals who blesses marriages and the birth of our children; merciless Hades, the unseen, unmentionable lord of the dead who dwells with his sister Demeter under the earth – we prefer to call on Plutus (the giver of wealth) to grant us the fruits of the Underworld; booming Poseidon, who rules the waves and brings earthquakes to the land – he is also lord of horses and keeps his own stables at the bottom of the sea; and the father of us all, gods and men, mighty Zeus who shakes the wide earth with his thunder.

But their father Cronus was worried about these children, as his own father Uranus had rightly been about Cronus, who had deposed him. Gaia and Uranus had warned Cronus that the same fate would befall him, that one day he too would be defeated by a child of his own. Whereas Uranus had pushed his babies back into Gaia's womb, Cronus, knowing how his mother had deceived Uranus, would not trust Rhea to keep them and he would therefore swallow them as they were born. But Rhea had a plan of her own; when she was expecting her sixth child, Zeus, she appealed to starry Uranus and Gaia to help her in avenging the wrongs of scheming Cronus. They told Rhea to come, when she felt that the baby was due, across the sea to the island of Crete. When Rhea felt the birth pangs, she travelled swiftly through the dark night until she found a hidden cave at Lyktos on Crete. There she left her baby in the care of Gaia and some nymphs, and back she rushed to

LEFT *Goya (1746–1828),* Cronus Devouring One of his Children. *The painter has emphasized the pre-civilized nature of the Titan, enjoying his cannibalistic meal against the dark backdrop of Chaos.*

Cronus, presenting him with a rock, bound in swaddling clothes, which he promptly swallowed.

Meanwhile Zeus grew into a strong young man, and the nymphs told him of his father's cruelty. Zeus married the Titan Metis (Thought) who slipped an emetic into Cronus' wine; a moment later up came the rock, which you can still see at Delphi, followed by the brothers and sisters of Zeus, first Poseidon, then Hades, Hera, Demeter and Hestia. Zeus also freed the Cyclopes; one day they would return his help by providing him with weapons of thunder and lightning against the Titans.

THE OLYMPIANS

The Children of Zeus

Zeus took the Oceanid Metis (Cunning Resourcefulness) as his first wife. Now Uranus and Gaia gave him the same advice that they had given Cronus, namely that he should beware his offspring. When one day he discovered that Metis was with child, he swallowed her, and prevented the birth of a son who would certainly have usurped his power; but the birth of a grey-eyed daughter Athene was allowed, and she had the wisdom of her father.

He then married slender Themis (Righteousness), Titan daughter of Uranus and Gaia, who gave birth to the three Horae sisters who watch over the affairs of mortals; they usher in the seasons of spring, summer and winter, and their names are Eirene (Peace), Eunomia (Order), and Dike (Justice). Three more daughters she had: Clotho, Lachesis and Atropos, the Fates who spin, measure out and cut the threads of our lives, apportioning both good and bad things.

Attracted to an Oceanid called Eurynome, who had her mother Tethys's lovely looks, he had by her the three Graces; they melt our flesh

with loving glances from their incredibly beautiful eyes; they fill our hearts with delight. They are aptly named Aglaea (Splendour), Euphrosyne (Good Cheer) and Thalia (Festivity).

With Demeter Zeus had white-armed Persephone, whom Hades snatched from the land of the living with her father's blessing.

By Mnemosyne he had nine daughters, the Muses; each wears a golden diadem to set off her lovely hair, inherited from their mother. They attend us at our feasts when we sing our songs of love and war. Their home is on Mount Pieria, near Olympus, but they also join musical Apollo at Mount Parnassus above Delphi, and have been seen on Helicon in Boeotia, anywhere where poets find their inspiration.

ABOVE The three Graces: *Pompeian wall-painting, 1st century AD. One of several versions of the group appearing as decorations on the walls of private Roman houses. The painting probably copied a lost Hellenistic sculpture and depicts the figures in a formal dance-like arrangement with flowers in their hands and hair.*

The king of gods and men finally married his sister Hera and she bore Ares the war god, Hebe goddess of youthful beauty who is cup-bearer to the Olympians and would one day marry the deified Heracles, and Eileithyia goddess of childbirth.

Without a woman's help was born Athene, who rouses our spirits to battle and leads our armies, loving the noise of the battlefield. Hera was furious and, as an act of revenge on her husband, produced Hephaestus the skilled craftsman of the Olympians.

Other Divine Births

The sea-goddess Amphitrite was loved by Poseidon the earth-shaker, but she refused his affections and fled to Atlas for protection. Poseidon in his despair sent his scouts our searching for her, and it was Delphinus who found her; as a reward, Poseidon placed him in the night sky as the constellation we call the Dolphin. Poseidon and Amphitrite had a powerful son Triton who lives with his parents in a house of gold at the bottom of the sea.

Aphrodite and Ares, the piercer of shields, had two formidable sons, Terror and Fear, who go into battle with their father the city destroyer,

breaking the tightest of battle-lines. Their daughter Harmonia married Cadmus the Theban king, and their own children were to meet tragedy after tragedy; Agave would one day kill her son Pentheus in the worship of Dionysus; Autonoe was the mother of Actaeon, a victim of his own hunting-hounds; and Polydorus was

RIGHT *Claude Lorrain (1600–82), Apollo and the Muses on Mount Helicon. The painter has depicted Greek Helicon in a misty northern landscape. The Classical temple probably adapted a Roman model.*

the ancestor of ill-fated Oedipus. They also had Semele who slept with Zeus and had a divine son, merry Dionysus of the golden locks, who one day would marry the auburn-haired Ariadne, daughter of King Minos of Crete; Zeus made her ageless and immortal for his son. The hero Heracles was born from another union between immortal and mortal, Zeus and Alcmene; after completing his labours, he was granted eternal life.

Maia the daughter of Atlas, climbed Olympus and had a glorious child by Zeus, Hermes the herald of the gods.

Zeus and Leto had two children, the loveliest of the gods in the heavens, Artemis and Apollo.

The Oceanid Perseis and Helius, tireless god of the Sun, had a daughter Circe the sorceress who would one day give brave sons to the hero Odysseus, and a son Aeetes, king of the land of the Golden Fleece. With another Oceanid, Idyia of the lovely cheeks, Aeetes had slender-ankled Medea.

Children of The Goddesses

The noble goddess of cereals Demeter lay with the hero Iasion in a fertile Cretan field that had been ploughed three times, an ancient ritual. Their son was the beneficent god Plutus (Agricultural Wealth) who walks the earth and gives riches and good fortune to anyone he meets.

Eos (Dawn) desired Cephalus, son of Hermes, and their son Phaethon, who was godlike in his beauty, attracted the attention of Aphrodite, lover of smiles; she carried him off to be a priest in her Syrian temple.

Aphrodite with the gleaming diadem made love to mortal Anchises of Troy and their son was heroic Aeneas (who would one day found the Roman people).

The daughters of Nereus, the Old Man of the Sea, had amorous adventures too. Thetis of the silvery feet was pursued by the mortal Peleus, changing shapes to avoid his grasp; their child was Achilles the lionheart.

19

BELOW *Jan Cossiers*
(1600–71),
Prometheus Carrying
Fire. *The rebellious*
Titan is shown bringing
the blazing light of
Olympus to dark earth;
the stolen fire is hidden
in a hollow fennel
stalk.

Prometheus, Champion of Mankind

The story of Prometheus the Titan appears in the earliest Greek literature and figurative vase-painting. His enduring popularity throughout the Classical period is surely due to his defiance of divine authority in order to provide mankind with the essentials of civilized life. It is no surprise that the Early Romantic artists such as the composer Beethoven and the poet Shelley became fascinated by Prometheus as a symbol of the superhuman struggle for justice. Here is Hesiod's account.

Iapetus was yet another Titan brother of Cronus; he went to the bed of the fine-ankled Oceanid Clymene, who bore him the strong-armed Atlas, whose punishment from Zeus one day would be to hold up the heavens from the earth; and Prometheus, such an intelligent schemer, like his uncle Cronus; and Epimetheus, his fool of a brother.

Prometheus fashioned clay objects, presenting the finished works to Olympian Zeus for approval. One day he invented man in the shape of Phaenon, a boy of beautiful features. Knowing Zeus' unbridled attraction to both boys and girls, Prometheus kept Phaenon from him. Zeus saw the youth from the clouds and sent his eagle down to snatch him. The king of the gods refused to hand back Prometheus' most prized creation and placed him in the heavens as the planet Jupiter. Prometheus defiantly made more from the same mould – thus the race of men came into being.

The gods demanded sacrifices of oxen from the men, more than they could give. Prometheus persuaded Zeus to accept only a part of each ox, but Zeus demanded that he be allowed to choose the best cut. Crafty Prometheus butchered an ox, wrapping the inedible bones and innards in tasty looking fat; the other portion consisted of the best meat, but was wrapped in unappetizing ox-hide. Zeus made the wrong choice, and being god of oaths, was compelled to receive the same tripe at every future sacrifice.

Zeus refused men the civilizing gift of fire; Prometheus stole it for his protégés, concealing it in the hollow stalk of fennel. As punishment, Zeus had Prometheus nailed to a cliff and every evening sent his eagle to peck at his liver, which each night regenerated, thus prolonging his agony. Thirty-thousand years later, Herakles shot the eagle with an arrow and freed Prometheus from his torment.

In the meantime life on earth had become too comfortable. Therefore Zeus commanded the smith-god Hephaestus to match Prometheus' beautiful creation with something that would plague men for ever. Hephaestus decided to create something that men would find beautiful, but discover to be bad at the core, just like the deceitful sacrifices which men offer gods. He created woman and called her Pandora. Grey-eyed Athene made a shining white dress for her, drew a beautiful embroidered veil over her head, but most wonderful of all was the golden crown which she placed on Pandora's lovely head; on this Hephaestus had hammered and chased all the animals of the earth and fish of the sea, and so lifelike they were that you could almost see them move and hear their different voices.

Pandora was presented to Epimetheus (whose name means 'think later'). His brother Prometheus (whose name means 'think first'), had warned him never to accept gifts from the gods. But Pandora came with a rich dowry and a sealed jar with the words 'DO NOT OPEN' written on its neck. Epimetheus immediately opened it and all the troubles of the world flew out; only Hope was left at the bottom.

BELOW The creation of Pandora; Athenian red-figure vase painting, early 5th century BC. (Left to right) Zeus, Hermes, Hephaestus, Pandora, with Eros floating above Pandora's head.

THE BATTLE OF THE TITANS AND OLYMPIANS

BELOW *Athene fights Alcyoneus and Gaia; relief sculpture from the altar of Zeus at Pergamon, early 2nd century* BC. *Athene wears the aegis (breastplate) with Medusa's head attached. Gaia emerges from the earth to help her son. Winged Nike (right) awards Athene the victory crown. The dramatic 'baroque' style with its contorted, emotional figures is typical of Hellenistic art.*

Beneath Mount Olympus is the plain of Thessaly, on the other side of which stands another mountain called Othrys; on high Othrys the proud race of giants, the Titans led by Cronus, had built a great fortress, from which they fought the gods whose leader was Zeus. The war had been going on for ten years, neither side gaining the upper hand. One day Zeus freed the Hecatoncheires, the three giants with 100 hands each, most terrifying children of Gaia and Uranus. He fed his new allies nectar and ambrosia, food of the gods, and as they sat and ate together with the Olympians, Zeus stood and addressed the three brothers, Cottus, Gyes and Obriareus:

'Now listen to me, children of Gaia and Uranus, and let me tell you what I really think. We have been fighting your brother and sister Titans for many years; the victory will bring us total power. Will you now repay us for giving you freedom after so many years spent beneath the earth in darkness? Let us see you making good use of those 100 hands by wielding many swords and spears against the Titans.'

Cottus immediately stood up and replied from one of his fifty heads:

'You are our friend indeed, great Zeus. You do not have to remind us of the time we have spent in our gloomy prison, humiliated by cruel Cronus, unable to put our strength to good use. We can see that you have great intelligence and profound understanding, which you have used to save the immortals from grave danger, and now you have brought the three of us out of darkness into light and we are eternally in your debt. To show our gratitude we will make sure that you will gain a final victory over the Titans; there will be terrible bloodshed and great slaughter on that day.'

LEFT *Giovanni Battista
Tiepolo (1693–1770)
Olympus. Zeus sits in
majesty on a cloud,
while Hermes performs
aerobatics above;
Aphrodite sits with
Eros (Cupid) aboard a
chariot pulled by her
sacred doves; Athene
appears below.
Tiepolo's skill at
decorating palatial
ceilings with divine
skyscapes is exhibited
here on canvas.*

The Olympian gods, sitting round the great table, applauded the speech and raising their cups of nectar, made a toast to their strange new allies. The thought of victory after so many years inspired a yearning for battle in their hearts and the Hecatoncheires led the charge across the plains of Thessaly to the Titan stronghold. They discarded the spears and swords given to them by the gods, finding them of little use against the strong walls built by the Titans. Instead they tore entire cliffs from the mountain and hurled these uncouth but effective missiles at the Titan defences. In their turn, the Titans retaliated, and never have the earth, sea and sky been so near to collapsing than on that day. Their battle-cries shook the very top of Mount Olympus and resounded down to the dark depths of Tartarus and way up again into the heavens; even the stars were shaking.

Zeus, seeing that his splendid palace, the work of Hephaestus, was in imminent danger of collapsing, grew angry and displayed his full powers for the first time. He was fearful to behold as he reached into the starry heavens for his thunderbolts. Out of the huge gates of Olympus he came, fury in his eyes, blinding sparks of lightning flashing around his majestic body as he strode across the plain. Nothing was safe from his destruction on that day; he left scorched footprints in the life-giving earth, and the forests crackled with fire as he passed. Soon the flames were everywhere, licking the flat earth and lashing out at the heavens; if you could have borne to look at it, you would have seen into the deepest parts of the chasm, so bright was the fiery glare, and intense the heat. There was a mighty crash as though Uranus had collapsed with all his weight on top of Gaia, and the winds came from all sides to magnify the might of Zeus. To tip the scales of the battle the Hecatoncheires took a rock in each hand, and soon the sky was darkened by 300 missiles, which hurtled down upon the Titans within their stronghold. They could no longer resist the terrible onslaught, and the gods chased them down the mountain and beneath the earth into dark Tartarus, which is as far below earth as heaven is above it – a bronze anvil, dropped from earth would take ten days to hit the bottom of Tartarus.

THE UNDERWORLD AND ITS INHABITANTS

Tartarus is like a huge jar enclosed in three layers of pitch darkness, with a stopper of bronze to keep the Titans from earth. Cottus, Gyes and valiant Obriareus stand guard over it; and inside they say there are violent

ABOVE *Joachim Patinir (c1480–1524) Charon Crossing the River Styx. Angel-like figures (left) escort the dead from the land of the living, with its fantastic crystal domes, to the banks of the River Styx. Charon ferries them to Hades (right), where Cerberus guards the gates; the fires and scenes of death together with the angels suggest a Christian vision of Hell. The painting is typical of the cool expansive landscapes of northern Renaissance artists.*

gusts, the only sensation in the terrifying darkness; even the gods do not like to think about the place. Nearby stands the gloomy house of Nyx (Night) with its thick black curtains. By day Nyx lives there, but at night she leaves it and greets her daughter Hemera (Day) whom she passes on her way to the house, which they share but where they can never be found at home together. While Hemera carries light around the earth, Nyx sits at home, brooding over her children, beautiful young Hypnos (Sleep) and his ugly elder brother Thanatos (Death). Helius never sees either of them: Hypnos moves quietly over sea and land, gentle and mild towards mankind; but Thanatos struts about at random, with heart of iron and merciless soul of bronze, destroying anyone he comes upon.

In a magnificent palace with silver columns supporting a roof of long rocks, lives Styx, the goddess who makes even the immortals shudder; for when there is a dispute among the gods on Olympus, or one of them is accused of speaking a lie, Zeus sends rainbow-bodied Iris down into the depths of the underworld to bring the great oath of the gods back from the river Styx (which they swear by). The water

enters the Styx from a great height, cascading down a high cliff, at the bottom of which Iris collects the water in a golden jug. Any god who breaks an oath sworn over that holy water, can expect to lie in a coma breathless for a year without touching his food of nectar or ambrosia; and that is only the beginning of his ordeal, for after his illness he is exiled from the snowy peak of Olympus. After nine years he can once again join the immortals at their meals.

ZEUS FIGHTS TYPHON

After Zeus had pushed the Titans out of heaven and earth, there was a brief time of peace, while the smouldering lands and forests tried to recuperate after the battle. But Gaia decided to have yet another child, this time with dark Tartarus, inspired by golden Aphrodite; his name was Typhon, and he is one of the most terrifying creatures, with 100 heads like snakes with flickering black tongues and sinister eyes glimmering with fire beneath the brows; but most remarkable were the different voices that could be heard from each head. You could sometimes hear the bellowing of a mighty bull, and at other times the roar of a wild lion, or the howling of a pack of hunting-dogs; and sometimes he would seem to utter in crystal tones for the ears of the gods, or they would all hiss together echoing in the surrounding hills. This proud son of Tartarus and Gaia had a high ambition, no less than to rule the heavens and the earth.

Luckily Zeus became aware of his scheming, and out he strode to defend Olympus a second time. Once more the earth and sky resounded with his thunder and even the dark violet sea was set alight as Typhon the giant fought Zeus the god with his fiery breath. Beneath the earth Hades himself trembled with fear, and Cronus

and the Titans down in Tartarus also heard the fearsome noise of fighting. Zeus stood on Olympus and reached into the heavens for his lightning and thunderbolts. Suddenly he leapt from the mountain down onto the monster's back, pummelling him with blow after blow. Typhon gradually weakened and as he hit the ground, his mother Gaia groaned under his huge weight. The land for miles around was scorched by the heat of his crippled body, in places it melted like tin when heated in crucibles by metalworkers, or when iron is smelted by the craft of Hephaestus. Before any more damage could be done, Zeus hurled the hefty body down into Tartarus, a fine companion for the Titans. Typhon brings violent winds and havoc to sailors at sea, and his typhoons are destructive to the work of men too; crops and flowers are uprooted by his gusts and the air is filled with dust.

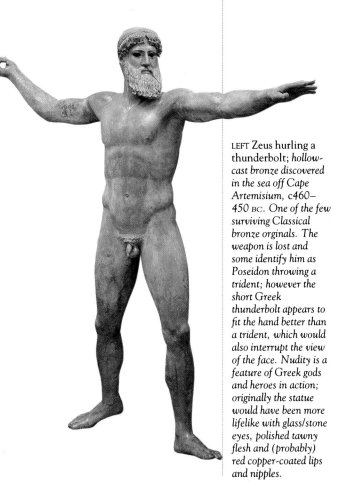

LEFT Zeus hurling a thunderbolt; *hollow-cast bronze discovered in the sea off Cape Artemisium, c460–450 BC. One of the few surviving Classical bronze orginals. The weapon is lost and some identify him as Poseidon throwing a trident; however the short Greek thunderbolt appears to fit the hand better than a trident, which would also interrupt the view of the face. Nudity is a feature of Greek gods and heroes in action; originally the statue would have been more lifelike with glass/stone eyes, polished tawny flesh and (probably) red copper-coated lips and nipples.*

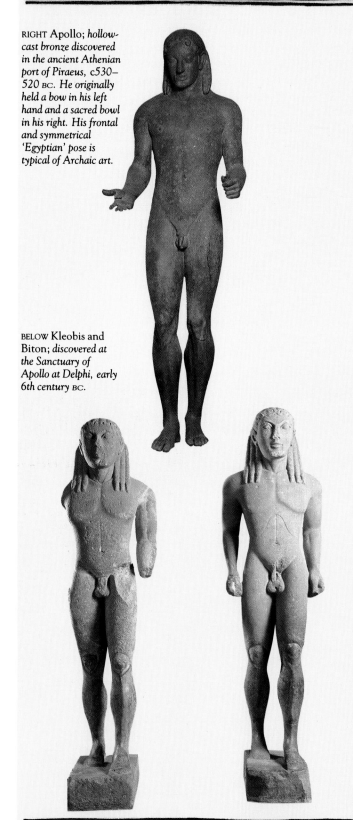

RIGHT Apollo; hollow-cast bronze discovered in the ancient Athenian port of Piraeus, c530–520 BC. He originally held a bow in his left hand and a sacred bowl in his right. His frontal and symmetrical 'Egyptian' pose is typical of Archaic art.

BELOW Kleobis and Biton; discovered at the Sanctuary of Apollo at Delphi, early 6th century BC.

GREEK SCULPTURE

Stylistic periods of Greek Art:
c650–490 BC: ARCHAIC
c490–450 BC: EARLY CLASSICAL
c450–400 BC: HIGH CLASSICAL
c400–323 BC: LATE CLASSICAL
c323–30 BC: HELLENISTIC

In prehistoric times, Greek artists had created images of gods and goddesses from tree-trunks and beaten metal. In the 7th century BC they learnt from the Egyptians how to carve marble statues; this tradition continued throughout the Classical period. In the 6th century BC they also learnt the technique of casting large, hollow bronze statues. During the Archaic period there was little physical distinction between gods and men. The statues were used as offerings to the gods (male nudes for gods, draped females for goddesses) to stand around their temples; but were these representations of the god or the worshipper? They were also used as tomb monuments to commemorate the deceased. In the Archaic period, sculptors, painters and even potters and painters of vases begin to sign their work and to label figures with names, suggesting a degree of respect for their work by socially superior patrons, as well as a relatively high standard of literacy.

A pair of Archaic statues which can be identified are Kleobis and Biton; they were set up at Delphi in the early 6th century BC to commemorate the heroic deed of the two brothers. The Greek historian Herodotus tells us that their mother wished to attend the festival of Hera at Argos; as the temple was several miles away she asked her farmer husband for the use of his oxen to take her by cart, but he replied that they were needed in the fields. Therefore her two sons, Kleobis and Biton, offered to pull the cart. At the festival

their mother prayed at night to Hera to grant her sons the greatest of divine rewards; the next morning she woke to find them dead and their immortality was assured by the sending of these two marble statues to Delphi. The dedication is certain owing to the preserved inscription on the statue base.

By the 5th century BC these bronze and marble figures could represent both gods and men, and had reached a high degree of naturalism which always conformed to an ideal of beauty. The marble statues were always painted in increasingly lifelike colours. The bronzes were also more naturalistic than they now appear; they would be polished to a tawny, flesh-like surface with red copper lips and nipples, silver-coated teeth and realistic eyes of coloured stone. The gods are recognizable by their attributes: Apollo holds a bow, Athene wears armour, Zeus holds a thunderbolt, Poseidon a fish or trident.

ABOVE Poseidon, Apollo and Artemis; *from the Athenian Parthenon frieze, 447–432 BC. This slab comes from the east end, where the gods were shown presiding over the procession which decorated the rest of the 525-foot/160-metre frieze. The designer, probably Phidias, exhibits qualities typical of High Classical sculptors: a mixture of naturalism and idealism in drapery and anatomy; an avoidance of monotony by varying the poses and gestures of the figures.*

RIGHT Apollo Belvedere; *Roman marble copy of 4th-century* BC *original by Leochares. In the early 5th century* BC *sculptors broke away from the stiff symmetrical poses of the Archaic period and created standing statues in naturalistic 'relaxed' poses with the weight shifted onto one leg. The contrast between drapery and anatomy is typical of Late Classical art. The tree-trunk support would not have been necessary in the bronze original.*

RIGHT 'Varvakeion' Athene; *Roman marble copy of Phidias' lost 5th-century* BC *chryselephantine cult statue of Athene Parthenos (see opposite); discovered in Athens, 2nd century* AD. *Such Roman copies provide invaluable evidence for lost works and, combined with written descriptions, enable art historians to reconstruct the original statues.*

Mythical narratives generally require more than one figure and in the Classical period sculptors began to create statue groups in tableaux representing crucial moments in the stories. Religious buildings were often decorated with sculptures which also tended to represent myths. One of the most famous temples, the Parthenon at Athens, was decorated in the High Classical period with marble sculptures depicting several mythical subjects. The pediments contained 'in-the-round' sculptures representing the birth of Athene and her contest with Poseidon for the patronage of Athens; the 'metopes' (square slabs positioned above the external colonnade) were decorated in 'high relief' with scenes of Lapiths fighting Centaurs, Greeks fighting Amazons, gods fighting giants and Greeks fighting Trojans: all symbolic of the conquest of barbarians by civilized Greeks. The low-relief frieze ran around all external sides of the inner temple and represented the Panathenaic procession at the climax of which a new gown was placed on the old wooden status of Athene in the presence of the gods. Within the temple stood a huge chryselephantine (gold and ivory) statue of Athene designed by Pheidias.

These statue types continued into the later Classical and Hellenistic periods, but styles changed: more sensual, earthly figures were created in the 4th century BC while the Hellenistic period saw a wider range of subject, from babies to drunken old women, as well as a more dramatic and 'realistic' style. These changes reflected the tastes of the new royal patrons, who required visually exciting statues of new subjects in novel poses to decorate their palaces – for the first time perhaps artists were producing 'art for art's sake'.

LEFT Athene Parthenos; model reconstructed from ancient copies (see bottom left) and literary descriptions, 447–432 BC. Phidias' cult statue (now lost) was designed as an impressive monument to the Greek victory over the Persians; it was built on a wooden frame with ivory for the flesh and gold for the drapery; it stood about 11 metres tall. The shield was decorated with reliefs depicting Greeks fighting Amazons and Gods fighting Giants, the sandals with Lapiths fighting Centaurs – all symbolic of the triumph of civilization – Nike (Victory) stood on Athene's right hand and on the base the birth of Pandora was depicted. The sculpture is typical of High Classical standing female figures with its weight shifted to one leg and the other bent at the knee. A pool of water was placed before the statue to reflect the gold and moisturize the ivory. Phidias was accused of embezelling the gold and it had to be removed and weighed. It was also said that he portrayed himself as one of the Greeks on the shield which, if removed, would bring the whole statue crashing to the floor.

TWO

The Olympian Gods

RIGHT *Zeus and Hera;*
black-figure lekythos
(funerary oil-vase)
discovered in the
Athenian Agora
(market-place), mid
6th century BC. *Hera*
ties a wreath round the
head of Zeus who
wields his thunderbolt.
The gods are
welcoming Heracles
(other side of vase) into
Olympus, the entrance
to which is marked by a
temple column.

The Olympian gods traditionally number twelve: Zeus, Hera, Athene, Hephaestus, Ares, Aphrodite, Apollo, Artemis, Demeter, Hestia, Poseidon and Hermes. Dionysus often replaces Hestia in the ancient lists. Other residents on Mount Olympus include Heracles after his deification; his wife Hebe, daughter of Hera, cup-bearer to the gods and goddess of youth; Eros, boy god of sexual passion, companion to Aphrodite; Iris, a Titaness, messenger to Zeus then later to Hera, appearing to men as a rainbow; Ganymede, cup-bearer to Zeus. Hades remained in the Underworld.

After his victory over Typhon, Zeus apportioned the gods with their various realms and powers and they were forbidden to overreach themselves: thus Aphrodite, being a non-military love-goddess, was chided by Zeus for appearing on the Trojan battlefield, and only Hermes had access to Heaven, Earth and the Underworld. In literature, the divinities are given their own epithets or stock descriptions, for example: Zeus 'Gatherer of Clouds', 'ox-eyed' Hera, Athene 'of the flashing eyes'. In the visual arts, they are recognized by their age, dress and attributes, though these are not consistent in early Greek art.

ZEUS

Son of Cronus and Rhea, he proved his superiority in single combat against Typhon and in the battle with the Titans and became king on Mount Olympus. After having a number of children with Titanesses, he married his sister Hera; although they had several important children, their marriage was far from happy, mainly owing to Zeus' tendency to lust after mortal women. A common pattern emerges in these relationships: Zeus is attracted to a woman and is compelled to visit her in disguise (his true appearance with thunder and lightning would destroy a human being); Hera discovers the affair and seeks revenge against her husband by punishing the woman or the offspring of the liaison.

Zeus (meaning 'to shine') was god of the sky in all its moods, from the clear bright light to the darkest storm. He administered justice and protected oaths sworn in his name. In art he appears as a long-haired (sometimes plaited up), mature and somewhat imposing figure; he is represented in heroic nudity as well as in full regalia; his attributes are his throne, sceptre, thunderbolt (not our modern zigzag design, but rather like an exploded fat cigar), diadem and eagle. His most important sanctuary was Olympia where all Greek states were entitled to compete in the games held in his honour every four years. A rich temple was built there in the 5th century BC which housed the gold and ivory statue of the god seated on his throne; it was made by Pheidias and became one of the Seven Wonders of the World.

HERA

A daughter of Cronus and Rhea, Hera was one of the gods to be swallowed by Cronus; when she was vomited back up by the Titan, she did not join the battle with her brothers and sisters against the giants, but was put into the care of Oceanus and Tethys. She became the permanent wife of Zeus after his relationships with other goddesses, and became the guardian of marriage and childbirth; her character in the myths reflects this role and she is constantly venting her anger at her husband's infidelities. Her children by Zeus were Ares, Hebe (guardian of youthful beauty and divine cup-bearer) and Eileithyia (goddess of childbirth); in angry response to the birth of Athene without a mother, Hera bore Hephaestus without a father.

In art Hera is depicted as a mature woman, sometimes with an elaborate crown and sceptre and holding a wedding veil aside from her head. Her most important cult centre was at Argos.

ATHENE

Virgin goddess of war as well as the arts and crafts and in later times of general wisdom, Athene had an extraordinary birth. Zeus had been warned by his grand-parents, Gaia and Uranus, that his first wife, Metis,

LEFT The birth of Athene; *red-figure pelike (possibly a container for perfumed oil) discovered in an Etruscan tomb at Vulci, early 5th century BC. A miniature Athene, fully armed, pops out of Zeus's head which has been split by Hephaestus' axe. The smith-god wears the craftsman's short tunic. Poseidon holds his trident; Zeus his sceptre.*

would have a son who would overthrow Zeus as he had his own father. Zeus therefore swallowed Metis, who was pregnant, and forgot all about her until one morning he awoke with a terrible headache and a rattling sound in his head. Hephaestus was called in to crack open Zeus' skull to see what the trouble way; the smith-god obliged and out jumped Athene in full armour – she became Zeus' favourite. Her titles 'Promachos' (the Champion) and 'Ergane' (Worker) reflected her dual role as a goddess of war and everyday work.

In art she appears as a tall, slim, noble woman with helmet, spear and shield and her special breastplate, the aegis, decorated with the head of the Gorgon Medusa, worn over a long tunic. Her main sanctuary was on the Acropolis at Athens where an ancient wooden image of her was worshipped in the Erechtheion, while Pheidias constructed a huge gold and ivory statue of the goddess for the magnificent Temple of Athene Parthenos ('Virgin'), called the Parthenon. The

RIGHT Mourning Athene; *votive relief from the Athenian Acropolis, c470 BC. Athene probably contemplates a tombstone which lists the Athenians who died in the Persian wars. Traces of blue pigment were found on the background. The goddess wears her helmet and peplos dress, belted at the overfold; she carries her spear but has removed her aegis (breastplate).*

Panathenaic Games were held in her honour every year, while every four years there was a special festival during which a new tunic was placed on the old wooden statue.

Long ago the Athenians had built up a prosperous city and desired a god to protect them. Both Poseidon and Athene wanted the honour and began to fight for it. The Athenians suggested a more peaceful way of settling the dispute: whichever of the two gods gave them the greatest gift would be awarded the city. Poseidon went first and thrust his trident into the Acropolis rock to bring forth a salt-water pool which threatened to flood the city; the Athenians protested that their rich farmland would be spoilt and asked Athene to produce a more useful gift. Athene struck the rock with her spear and immediately an olive tree sprouted; the Athenians realised that its fruit would provide them with oil for cooking, lighting and perfume and awarded the city to her protection. The marks of the trident and the sacred olive tree remained for centuries.

On one occasion Athene was bringing a huge rock to plant as a natural defensive barrier for Athens; Hephaestos saw her coming and attempted to make love to her as she flew towards the walls. She managed to fend him off and the rock fell to the ground to become the conical hill Lykabettos, while his seed fell onto the Acropolis and Erichthonius, the future King of Athens was born. Athene not only fought with the Athenians but accompanied many Greek heroes on their adventures.

POSEIDON

S̲on of Rhea and Cronus, god of the sea, earthquakes and horses, Poseidon received dominion over the sea when he drew lots with his brothers Zeus and Hades. His adventures often resemble those of Zeus, involving the

RIGHT Poseidon; *red-figure wine-cup painted by Oltos, late 6th century BC. Vase-painters often painted figures in the actual bowl of wine-cups, which would generally become visible as the person drank. Poseidon, seen here with his trident and fish as attributes, would thus have appeared running through a sea of wine. The signature around the border is that of the potter: Kachrylioni epoiesen ('Kachrylion made this').*

seduction of mortal women in the guise of animals, including a ram, a dolphin and a bird; and like Zeus, he also fell in love with men, taking Pelops to Olympus as his lover and presenting him with winged horses to win a chariot-race to obtain his wife; Pelops gave his name to the Peloponnese. Poseidon was constantly fighting for dominion of places on the land including Athens, which he lost to his niece Athene, and Corinth, where Helius received the hill of Acrocorinth and Poseidon was given the Isthmus which forms the bridge to Attica. An important sanctuary was dedicated to him at the Isthmus. In art he is similar to Zeus, perhaps lacking his more domineering attitude, and identifiable by his trident; sometimes he holds a sea-creature.

ARTEMIS

Daughter of Leto and Zeus and sister of Apollo, Artemis, like Athene, was a virgin goddess; she was given the wild areas outside city walls as her realm where she both hunted and protected the wild animals; she was also goddess of childbirth. Her encounters with men generally involve the administering of cruel punishments for their attempts to rape or spy on her. In art she appears as a beautiful huntress, usually in short tunic and bearing quiver and bow; in later art she can appear with the crescent moon on her head – a sign of her lunar associations.

When King Agamemnon was about to lead the Greek fleet to Troy to recapture his brother's wife Helen, who had been abducted by Paris, he stupidly boasted that he was a better hunter than Artemis. She punished him by refusing winds for his sailing ships unless he sacrificed his young daughter Iphigeneia to the goddess. The girl was taken to the altar but Artemis took pity on her and replaced her with a deer, carrying her away to be her priestess in the land of the barbarian Taurians where she would sacrifice all visiting strangers to Artemis.

APOLLO

Son of the Titaness Leto by Zeus, and brother of Artemis, Apollo was born on the island of Delos which remained sacred to him. While still a boy, Apollo journeyed to Delphi where he killed a huge snake called Python and took control of the Pythian oracle. He appeared as a dolphin to Cretan

LEFT Artemis of Versailles; Roman marble copy of 4th-century BC Greek original. The virgin goddess is here portrayed with short tunic and quiver while a sacred stag runs beside her. The sculpture reflects her dual role as both hunter and protector of wild animals.

RIGHT Apollo
'Sauroctonos'
(Lizard-Slayer);
*Roman marble copy of
4th-century* BC *Greek
original by Praxiteles.
The god is poised to
throw a dart at a lizard
as it climbs the tree.
The softness of the flesh
is typical of Praxiteles'
treatment of marble;
also Praxitelean is the
sinuous pose.*

BELOW RIGHT Apollo;
*Roman wall-painting,
1st century* AD. *Apollo
appears with his
attributes of lyre (god
of music) and quiver
(the hunter).*

sailors and took them to Delphi,
ordering them to guard his oracle and
build a temple to Apollo Delphinius
(of the Dolphin). Apollo and Artemis
defended the honour of their mother
when Niobe, Queen of Thebes,
boasted that she had more beautiful
children: they shot the Niobids with
their arrows.

Apollo was god of prophecy and
healing, and became associated with
music and cultural activities; he was
worshipped as a rational god, defend-
ing intellectual pursuits, the opposite
of Dionysus. He had many affairs with
both male and female mortal lovers.
In art he appears as a beardless handsome youth with long hair, often
plaited up; he holds a bow, lyre or his
sacred laurel branch.

35

ARES

Only son of Zeus and Hera, Ares was the god of war. He appears in art as an ordinary Greek warrior, with helmet, shield, sword and spear. His association with warfare is far from glamorous: generally we see him generating as much trouble as he can on the battlefield to cause the maximum bloodshed on both sides. His fellow Olympians do not care for him, apart from Aphrodite, who was his lover. On one occasion Hephaestus left Olympus and stayed for a while on the island of Lemnos. His wife Aphrodite called Ares into her bed, but Hephaestus had hung a net of fine wire over his bed, which fell upon them; they became completely tangled and Hephaestus invited all the other Olympians to laugh at the expense of the god of war and goddess of love. The smith god let them go free and Aphrodite returned to Cyprus and Ares returned to Thrace, a centre for his worship.

APHRODITE

The most famous account of the birth of the goddess of erotic love is that she appeared out of the sea-foam surrounding the severed genitals of Uranus; her name means 'born from foam'. Homer makes her a daughter of Zeus and the Oceanid Dione. Likewise Eros, the god of sexual desire, is her son by Ares in many accounts, though Hesiod has him welcoming the goddess ashore at her birth. Many Greeks associated her with Eastern love goddesses such as Ishtar; these were also war goddesses and this might explain Aphrodite's links with Ares, god of war. Her husband on Olympus was the lame god Hephaestus.

In art she appears at first as an attractive young woman, wearing pretty clothes and often holding a flower and a dove. Her most famous statue was made by Praxiteles for her shrine on the island of Kos, but when it was unveiled the town council rejected it, shocked by its nudity. The people of Knidos bought it for their sanctuary to the goddess, placing her in a romantically positioned circular temple. The temple, which became one of the most important cult centres of the goddess, was recently discovered by the aptly named Professor Love; the statue has long since disappeared, but its base and a Greek inscription telling us the artist and subject were found. She stood with her back to the setting sun and the sea. There was a story that a man, lusting after the statue, made love to it one night; this story emphasizes her physical sexual presence in antiquity rather than the more romantic view that developed later.

The depiction of Aphrodite as a beautiful mature woman preparing to bathe influenced all later representations of the goddess. She regularly appears with Eros, who is symbolized in early art as a beautiful youth with long wings and hair, holding the bow and gold-tipped arrows with which he pierces the hearts of lovers. In later art he multiplies into many children (Erotes or Cupids) with short wings, precursors of Renaissance 'putti'.

Aphrodite had both mortal and immortal lovers. Hermes was rejected by her, so Zeus sent his eagle to snatch her sandal and take it to Hermes, who would not return it until she had submitted. Their son was the beautiful youth Hermaphroditus with whom the Naiad Salmacis fell in love whilst he was bathing in her spring. As they made love, she clung to him so fast that their bodies fused into one. In art Hermaphroditus appears as a woman with male genitals.

HEPHAESTUS

HERMES

Hera probably produced this son without a father in retaliation to Zeus who had given birth to Athene without a mother. Hephaestus was rejected by Hera because of his lameness; she threw him out of Olympus into Oceanus where Thetis rescued him. When he grew up he punished his mother by making her a magical golden throne, but when she sat on it she found herself stuck fast. The gods tried to persuade Hephaestus to return to Olympus and forgive his mother; he refused until Dionysus gave him wine and led him back drunk on an ass to the great mirth of his fellow Olympians.

Hephaestus was associated with fire and the crafts of blacksmithing and metalwork and his workshop was thought to be beneath volcanoes such as Etna in Sicily. In art he often appears in a craftsman's short tunic, holding a double axe or a pair of blacksmith's tongs; his lameness is sometimes suggested by his leaning on a crutch. His temple in the Agora at Athens was close to potters' workshops and contained statues of both himself and Athene who was also associated with crafts.

Offspring of Zeus and one of the Pleiades, Maia, Hermes was born in a cave on Mount Cyllene in Arcadia. He was a precocious child and, on the very day of his birth, he climbed out of his cradle and killed a tortoise outside his cave and, using the shell as a sound-box and sheepgut for strings, invented the lyre. Later the same day, Hermes stole cattle belonging to Apollo and led them back to his cave, where he lay down in his cradle pretending innocence. Apollo eventually caught up with the thief (Hermes was later a god of thieves) and demanded the lyre in place of the cattle, in return for which he made Hermes god of herds and herdsmen. When he grew

BELOW Hephaestus and Thetis; Roman wall-painting from Pompeii, 1st century AD. Thetis sits in the smith-god's workshop and waits for the completion of her son Achilles' new armour. The shield is held up for inspection and the goddess is reflected in its polished surface; the helmet is still being hammered. Thetis is portrayed as a noble matron while Hephaestus wears the craftsman's tunic and skullcap.

RIGHT Hermes with
the infant Dionysus;
Praxiteles, 4th century
BC. This rare original
Greek marble by a
known artist was
discovered in the
Temple of Hera at
Olympia. Hermes is
depicted carrying baby
Dionysus to the
nymphs on Mount
Nysa and teases him
with a bunch of grapes
(now lost). The
contrast of drapery
with anatomy and the
sinuous pose and soft
flesh are typical of Late
Classical sculpture.

up, Zeus made him the messenger of
the gods; only Hermes was allowed
free passage between Olympus, the
Earth and the Underworld and he
escorted dead Greeks to the ferryman
Charon, who for a small coin would
carry the dead across the river Styx to
Hades.

Hermes, like Apollo, had many
love affairs. There is argument as to
the mother of his most famous son
Pan, who became god of shepherds.
In art, Pan appears as a lusty human
figure, sometimes with goats' legs and
horns and sometimes with goat's head
and human body; he often plays the
rustic pan-pipes. Hermes appears with
his *kerykeion*, a magic wand entwined
with snakes which gives him access to
all places. He is often bearded and
wears traveller's clothes, including a
sun-hat, short tunic and cloak; his
hat and boots are sometimes winged
for flight.

BELOW *Peter Paul
Rubens (1577–1640),
Artemis and her
Nymphs Attacked by
Pan with Satyrs.
Artemis (right) hurls
an arrow at lusty Pan
(left), who has come
with satyrs to molest
the virgin goddess while
she is out hunting with
her nymphs.*

DEMETER,
PERSEPHONE AND
HADES

Daughter of Cronus and Rhea, Demeter, goddess of corn and fertility, was seduced on earth by a prince called Iasion; their children were Plutus (Wealth) and Philomelus, who was made into the constellation Bootes ('the wagon'), which he invented. Zeus killed Iasion with a thunderbolt for presuming to love a goddess; Zeus then made love to Demeter himself and she bore a daughter named Persephone. Hades, brother of the Olympians and god of the Underworld, asked Zeus for Persephone as his wife. Zeus agreed, but, thinking that Demeter would not accept the match as she would lose her daughter forever to the Underworld, assisted Hades in Persephone's abduction. He asked Gaia to send up many lovely flowers near where Persephone dwelt; whilst she was picking them with her friends, Hades came up from the Underworld in a chariot and took the poor girl back with him. Demeter searched the world for many days and nights in the guise of a mortal. At every town she visited, she told men the secrets of the harvest; one of these towns, Eleusis, became a centre for her mystery cult. Demeter threatened famine to the earth unless her daughter was returned; but Persephone had eaten several pomegranate seeds which meant that she would have to stay in Hades for one-third of the year, during which period Demeter refused to allow the crops to grow. Festivals were held for the return of Persephone every spring. At Eleusis, Demeter lent her winged chariot, drawn by dragons, to the youth Triptolemus; he was to use it every year to scatter seed over the earth. In art, mother and daughter sometimes wear crowns and carry torches or ears of corn.

LEFT *Sir Edward Coley Burne-Jones (1833– 98), The Rape of Proserpine (1883–4); pencil drawing, touched with orange and red chalk. Hades emerges from the Underworld through a chasm in a four-horse chariot. Winged figures bear Persephone (Proserpina) away from her friends who tear their hair in grief. A many-headed snake appears from the cleft.*

RIGHT Demeter, Triptolemos and Persephone, *relief from Eleusis, Greece, c40–30 BC. Demeter, holding a sceptre, hands ears of corn (originally added in metal) to the young Triptolemos; Persephone holds a torch.*

DIONYSOS

Also known as Bacchus, the god of wine and vegetation, his mortal mother was Semele of Thebes, whom Zeus had taken as a lover. Jealous Hera appeared to Semele in the guise of her old nurse and dared her to demand that Zeus appear in his real form. Semele was incinerated by his thunderbolt, but Zeus salvaged the unborn boy and sowed him into his thigh; a few months later Dionysus was born and given to Hermes to entrust to the care of nymphs on Mount Nysa. When he grew up these nymphs became his female devotees, the Maenads. Hera drove him mad and he fled to the east where the oriental earth goddess Cybele cured him. He then returned to Greece, establishing his cult in different places and proved to the world that his father was Zeus.

In Classical art he appears as a beautiful youth with long hair and a thyrsos, a wand bound with ivy and topped with a pine cone; round his head he wears an ivy wreath and often carries an upturned wine cup. In later art he becomes increasingly effeminate in appearance.

His female followers, the Maenads, are human in form, but carry thyrsoi and wear skins from the animals they have slaughtered during the rites; often they wear ivy or even snakes for headbands. His male followers, the Satyrs,

RIGHT Dionysus, *Roman wall-painting, 1st century* AD. *The god holds his thyrsus and wears his ivy crown. In late Greek and Roman art the god appears increasingly effeminate; here he has the large hips and small breasts of a Classical female nude.*

appear as men with horses' tails,
pointed ears, and erect penises, signs
of the irrational animal nature that is
freed by the worship of Dionysus; we
often see them drinking or in lusty
pursuit of Maenads.

HESTIA

The eldest child of Cronus and
Rhea, Hestia guarded hearth, fire,
house, family and community. She
remained a virgin goddess, though
both Poseidon and Apollo had wished
to marry her. She rarely appears in art
and has few shrines, her home being
at the hearth.

ABOVE AND LEFT Satyrs
drinking; Athenian
red-figure psykter
(wine-cooler)
discovered in an
Etruscan tomb at
Cerveteri, painted by
Douris in the early 5th
century BC. The
psykter was filled with
ice and placed in wine
to cool it. The potter
balanced the vase so
that it floated at the
base-line of the figure-
scene. The drinker
could spin it round and
the satyrs would appear
to dance on the wine.
The satyrs pour wine
from rustic animal-
skins as well as civilized
pottery vases,
representing the use of
wine to bring out man's
animal nature at the
urban symposium
(drinking-party).

BELOW Introduction of Heracles to Olympus; *Athenian black-figure* oinochoe *(wine-jug) by the Amasis Painter, mid 6th century* BC. *In black-figure pottery, female flesh is often painted white to contrast with the darker, tanned male flesh; white flesh was a sign of rich women who did not often go outside of the house. The only other added colour was purple, seen here on Hermes' cloak and hat and on Athene's shield device (the owl was her sacred bird). Details of embroidered drapery and anatomy are incised through the black 'paint' before firing. The signature between Athene and Hermes reads* Amasis m'epoiesen *('Amasis made me').*

GREEK PAINTING

Ancient writers speak of renowned easel painters, but unfortunately none of their originals have survived. Mythical scenes formed a large part of their output; Roman interior decorators often painted copies of them, and surviving examples give us some idea of their original quality and style. By the Late Classical period painters had broken away from the Egyptian pictorial style with its flat images, and were using changing hues of colour and light and shadow effects to suggest solid figures within a three-dimensional space; this technique of 'chiaroscuro' had to be rediscovered by Italian Renaissance painters.

From the Archaic period onwards the vases used by Greeks for their symposia were painted with mythical scenes. There were two main styles: 'black-figure', in which the images were black silhouettes incised with details of dress and anatomy; and 'red-figure', in which the figures were reserved in the red of the oxidized clay and their details were painted in with a brush. The applied black 'pigment' was a refined version of the clay of the vase. The clay was shaken in water and left for a few days; fine metallic elements were held in suspension in the water and a paste was produced by evaporation; this iron-rich paste was used as the 'paint'. During firing the iron in the clay

was oxidized to become red iron oxide; the potter then closed the air supply and the resulting carbon monoxide turned the iron oxide into black ferrous oxide. For the final stage oxygen was allowed back into the kiln and the ordinary clay of the vase turned back to red iron oxide whilst the iron rich 'paint' remained black.

Black-figure vases first appear in the Archaic period and continue into the Classical period; the silhouetted figures are effective against the red clay background, but are flat and unnaturalistic, with profile legs and heads and unrealistic frontal eyes and torsoes. Red-figure vases appear in the Late Archaic period (c530 BC); this technique allows for a more naturalistic representation with light figures spotlighted against the black background; drapery and anatomical lines are now painted with the more fluid brush and this allows the painters to produce apparently three-dimensional figures. Three-quarter views of figures and profile eyes appear for the first time in the history of art. The Archaic and Classical artists relied on simple gestures and the viewer's knowledge of the myth rather than the overt expressions of emotion which were features of Hellenistic art.

The most popular scenes were not surprisingly Dionysiac. Other myths went in and out of fashion; Heracles was popular at the time of the tyrants during the Archaic period, but representations of Theseus were popular during the Classical period of democracy. Theseus, who had saved the Athenian youths from the Minotaur, was regarded as a democratic hero; Heracles who had risen above his fellow men and become a god would have been associated with tyrannical aspirations. It would therefore appear that, as in literature, the myths were not purely decorative, but could reflect political and social changes.

LEFT Selene and Endymion; *Roman wall-painting from a Pompeian house, 1st century* AD. *In the 1st century* AD *it was fashionable for Romans to decorate the walls of their houses with frescoes giving the illusion of an art gallery. Copies of earlier Greek 'Old Masters' (collected by connoisseurs) would be* painted in the centres of the walls as if the original easel-paintings were hanging there. In this painting 'windows' appear on either side of the painting to give the impression of a townscape outside: the perspective colonnades increase the illusion. The 'easel-painting' depicts Selene, head surrounded by the moon, approaching her sleeping lover Endymion. These paintings provide valuable information about the Greek easel-paintings, none of which have survived. In particular, they exhibit the 'chiaroscuro' (light and shade) technique, invented by Greek painters around 400 BC to create realistic three-dimensional effects.

BELOW Athene; *Athenian red-figure amphora, early 5th century* BC. *The red-figure technique allowed the painter to produce a more naturalistic image with* anatomy and drapery lines painted with a brush. This also facilitated the painting of three-quarter views and foreshortened limbs, as with Athene's left foot.

Italian Renaissance artists revived the Classical myths, but in most cases the only evidence they had for their representation in art was in literary descriptions of the lost ancient masterpieces. They would therefore 'reproduce' the paintings in their imagination and often dress the mythological figures in contemporary dress and locate them in Italian landscapes. The Florentine painter Botticelli made several paintings based on mythological subjects, including Aphrodite (Venus) subduing Ares (Mars) while her Erotes play with his armour. They lie in an Italian landscape and 'Venus' wears contemporary clothes. Renaissance artists and their patrons were highly sophisti-

cated in their interpretations of mythology and often read several meanings into the same image. Thus, *Venus and Mars* might also be seen as the marriage of Alexander the Great to the exotic princess Roxanne – the ancient writer Lucian describes the lost painting of this subject by Apelles and refers to 'Erotes' playing with the divine king's armour. Botticelli's Erotes are more like little horned devils, perhaps suggesting a more Christian idea of the temptation of man by woman. There is no evidence that Botticelli himself named his painting *Venus and Mars*, and therefore any of these interpretations might be correct.

BELOW *Sandro Botticelli (1445–1510)*, Venus and Mars.

THREE

Tales of Greek Heroes

Apart from the legendary warriors of Homer's epic poems who fought at Troy, several heroes existed who were the central subjects of lengthy sagas. All exhibited super-human strengths, clearing the world of its troublesome monsters, and generally experienced a number of love affairs.

Heracles and Theseus were contrasted in both art and literature. As a boy, Heracles rejected his education and relied on sheer brute strength in his later encounters with men and monsters. He was deified at death and was later worshipped as a god by military men. Theseus was seen as an educated and civilized version of Heracles and became the hero of Athenian democracy in the 5th century BC. He performed similar super-human tasks as Heracles, but introduced more 'gentlemanly' fighting skills. In art Theseus appears short-haired and clean-shaven, while Heracles, easily recognized by his lion skin and club, sports long, shaggy hair and a beard. Perseus (meaning 'slayer-destroyer'), like Heracles, appears to have represented the earlier, more violent stage of Greek mythology. In art Perseus is usually depicted in the winged sandals and magic hat used on his quest for the head of Medusa.

HERACLES

As King and Queen of Tiryns and Mycenae Perseus and Andromeda had many children, but this tale concerns just two of their sons, Alcaeus and Electryon. Alcaeus had a son named Amphitryon, who married his cousin Alcmene, the daughter of Electryon. Amphitryon wanted to become king, but his uncle Electryon stood in his path so he murdered him; the attempted coup failed and Amphitryon and Alcmene were exiled. They travelled to Thebes where King Creon welcomed them. Alcmene would not sleep with Amphitryon until he had avenged her brothers who had been killed by pirates. He returned in triumph one night and they made love whilst he told her of his adventures. Imagine her surprise when the next day he walked in and told her the same stories all over again, as if for the first time. They called in Teiresias the prophet who told them that Zeus had visited Alcmene in the guise of her husband. Amphitryon was willing to forgive Alcmene, but problems arose when Alcmene became pregnant; the whole Theban court waited to see whether the child would be Amphitryon's or Zeus'.

Meanwhile on Olympus, Zeus boasted that a son of his was about to be born on earth who would be a great ruler. Hera, understandably angry and jealous, sent Eileithyia, goddess of childbirth, to delay Alcmene's labour and speed up the birth of Eurystheus, grandson of Perseus, and great-grandson of Zeus, to ensure his inheritance of the throne of Tiryns in place of Alcmene's child. The next day Alcmene gave birth to twin sons, named Iphicles and Heracles, but no one was able to say whether either was the god's progeny. The problem was solved when Hera sent two snakes into the babies' cots as they slept. Iphicles screamed but, to the surprise of Amphitryon and Alcmene, little

LEFT *Heracles in the garden of the Hesperides; Roman wall-painting from the villa at Oplontis, 1st century AD. A sun-tanned Heracles carries his club and looks up at the golden apples; the special tree is marked with a ribbon.*

LEFT The infant Heracles strangling the snakes; *Roman wall-painting from the House of the Vettii, Pompeii, 1st century AD. Heracles has laid aside his tiny baby's club to deal with the snakes. His mortal father Amphitryon raises his hand in wonder at the child's strength, whilst the eagle reminds us of his real father Zeus. This might be a copy of a well known lost original of the scene by the 4th-century BC Greek painter Zeuxis, the inventor of the 'chiaroscuro' technique which is fully apparent in this painting; note the shading and highlights on Amphitryon.*

Heracles took the snakes by the necks and strangled them; there was no doubt that this was a son of Zeus.

Heracles received the normal royal education: his step-father taught him to drive the chariot, and various experts were called in to teach him to fence, wrestle and use the bow and arrow; but Heracles showed little interest in these gentlemanly skills, finding that it was quicker and easier to dispatch his opponent with one blow of the fist or a swing of his club. This rather worried his mortal parents, and they thought that some training in the arts would make him behave a little more gracefully. Orpheus's brother Linus, himself a wonderful musician and teacher, was called in to give Heracles music lessons. Heracles proved to be a slow learner and one day Linus lost his temper and struck him; Heracles angrily brought his lyre down on Linus's head killing him instantly; the boy did not know his own strength, nor where it came from.

Amphitryon thought it would be sensible to send him away from the city for a while and Heracles spent many happy summers on the royal cattle farm. In his spare time he would practise with his bow and arrow on the slopes of Mount Cithaeron; he never missed, but found that there were certain creatures whose skins could not be pierced with arrows, so Heracles would wrestle with them. However, there was one that eluded him, a lion that had been eating the flocks of Thespius, their royal neighbour. To get him in a good mood and to see how strong this young man really was before asking him to kill the lion, Thespius invited Heracles to supper and plied him with gallons of wine. That night Thespius sent all fifty of his daughters to his guest's room; the next morning each swore that Heracles had made love to them, but Heracles could not remember anything. On his way back to Thebes he killed the lion with his own bare hands. Nearing Thebes, he encountered some ambassadors on their way from Orchomenus in Minya to collect their annual tribute from Thebes; Heracles in his anger, cut off their noses and ears, and hanging them round their necks, sent them back home with what he called their tribute.

War followed and Heracles led the Thebans to victory. Creon rewarded him with his daughter Megara.

Heracles had been away on business and several years later on his return to Thebes found that Creon had been murdered by a Euboean called Lycus, who was about to execute Heracles' wife and their children. Heracles killed Lycus, but as he was embracing Megara, Hera never forgetting her grudge, brought a fit of madness upon him, and he killed both his wife and his children. Coming to his senses he saw with horror what he had done and took his impure body away from Thebes and walked to Delphi to seek advice from the Pythian Oracle. She pronounced that to atone for his crime, he must travel to Tiryns and ask King Eurystheus to set him ten trials of his strength and courage. Heracles turned to go with face downcast; humiliated that this weakling of a king, Eurystheus, who sat on the throne which he himself would have held if Hera had not tricked his father Zeus, was to have such power over his fate; but the Pythia called after him that if he suc-

ceeded in the ten labours he would achieve immortality. Heracles rose to the challenge and was impatient to begin the first of his labours.

1 *The Nemean Lion*

Heracles' euphoria faded, however, when he stood in Tiryns before the throne of his rival Eurystheus who smirked and demanded the pelt of the Nemean Lion, one of the monstrous sons of Orthus and Echidna, which had been ravaging the surrounding countryside. On his way to Nemea, Heracles stayed for the night in the hut of a peasant named Molorchus, who, when he heard what Heracles was attempting, offered a sacrifice to him. Heracles told his to delay the sacrifice for a month, after which if he had not returned, the sacrifice should be made to Heracles the Hero; but if he returned in triumph, the sacrifice must be made to Zeus the Saviour.

Molorchus pointed out the long path to the lion's cave and wished him luck. Fifteen days later Heracles could hear its distant roaring for several

RIGHT Heracles and the Nemean Lion; *black-figure* oinochoe *(wine-jug), late 6th century* BC. *Heracles has hung up his quiver and bow on a tree and wrestles with the lion.*

hours before he eventually found himself peering through the bushes at a cave with two entrances. Heracles strung his bow and, without making a sound, fitted an arrow; he then flung a rock against the nearest mouth of the cave. Immediately a lion, twice the size of the one he had strangled on mount Cithaeron, leapt out of the cave, roaring and spitting with rage at being disturbed. Heracles let his arrow fly and, true as ever, it found its mark between the eyes of the magnificent beast, but Heracles' heart sank as it bounced straight off again. 'What a wonderful warm and light coat of armour that pelt would make, if Zeus would help me to kill the lion!', thought Heracles. Zeus heard him from Olympus – they were all up there watching – and sent his warlike daughter, Athene of the flashing eyes, down to help. Unknown to Heracles, she gave him new courage and he stepped out into the open, rolling a stone in front of one of the entrances; he entered the other one and slew the lion, strangling it as easily as he had the snakes when he was a baby.

Meanwhile Molorchus was preparing to sacrifice to Heracles the dead hero, it being a month since Heracles had left him. Upon seeing the hero returning with the dead Nemean lion over his shoulder, Molorchus praised Zeus and burnt the sacrifice to the Gatherer of Clouds, reserving the meat for a night of feasting and drinking in celebration of Heracles' victory. The local peasants joined them in dancing well into the night; at last they could work in the fields without fear of the monster.

Eurystheus was annoyed when Heracles entered Tiryns in triumph; he was expecting never to see him again and what is more was terrified when he saw the lion which looked as if it might spring to life at any moment. Eurystheus jumped into a storage jar to hide; Heracles could not conceal his amusement and Eurystheus angrily vowed that Heracles would not be laughing when he heard what his next labour was to be. Hera rewarded the

lion's vain attempts to defy Heracles by setting it as the stars in the heavens known as the constellation Leo.

II The Hydra

The Hydra was the half-sister of the Nemean Lion, spitefully chosen by Eurystheus as the object of Heracles' second labour as he knew that the Hydra would be yearning to avenge her relative's death. The Hydra had the venomous nature of her father Typhon, who lay crushed by Zeus under Mount Etna, breathing his fires. Heracles left Tiryns, wearing the magnificent pelt of the Nemean lion, its scalp protecting his head like a hood, and as soon as he was clear of the gates, Eurystheus had them bolted and shouted after him from the ramparts that he was to leave any further trophies outside the city walls. Heracles laughed and went on his way in high spirits, accompanied by his nephew Iolaus, who had volunteered to be his charioteer.

The Hydra lived in a pool formed by the freshwater spring Amymone at Lerna. The spring had once been crystal clear and a source of drinking water for the people of Lerna. Now it was polluted and they had to draw their water from a well some distance away, and this meant passing by the Hydra's lair; many of them never returned, finding themselves in one of the jaws of the monster, who would lie in wait for them with its accomplice, Cancer the crab, who would run out and grab the feet of unsuspecting travellers. Heracles approached the pool without fear and fired burning arrows into the cave behind the pool where the Hydra was supposed to live. Out she came, and Heracles was surprised at seeing so many heads, for no one had seen the monster and lived to tell the tale. He did not have time to reflect and found himself hacking away at its heads with his sword; but for every head lost, it immediately grew two more, and he found himself cornered when the giant crab sallied out to bite his ankles. He called to his charioteer Iolaus for help, and the clever youth brought burning torches with which he cauterized the wounded necks as Heracles removed the heads. At last only its huge central head was left; Heracles cut it off with a final blow and buried it beneath a large stone which still lies beside the road outside Lerna. He dipped his arrows into the dead Hydra's poisonous blood and returned to Tiryns in triumph, but Eurystheus refused to acknowledge the labour as one of the ten as Iolaus had helped the hero.

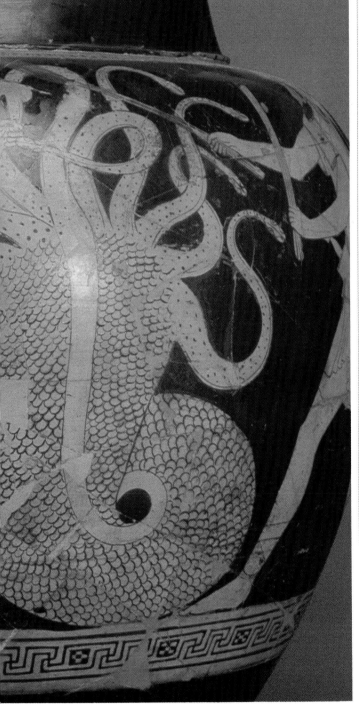

LEFT Heracles and the Hydra; *Athenian red-figure* stamnos *(wine-jar) by the Syleus Painter, early 5th century* BC. *Heracles (left) has laid aside his club to sever the snake-heads while his companion Iolaus cauterizes the open wounds with torches.*

III *The Cerynitian Hind*

For his third labour, Heracles was ordered to capture the golden-horned deer known as the fabulous Cerynitian Hind. The problem for Heracles was that he was to bring it back alive; moreover, the hind was sacred to the goddess Artemis. It had last been seen in the woods around Oenoe in Argolis, a short journey for Heracles. He tracked it down after a year and had little trouble dragging it away with nets. But on the way to Tiryns he encountered Artemis and Apollo who demanded that he return the deer. Heracles blamed Eurystheus, and they let him pass, so long as he did not harm the creature.

IV *The Erymanthian Boar*

Eurystheus now tried to exhaust Heracles, immediately sending him back down to Arcadia to capture alive a huge boar which was terrorizing the shepherds on Mount Erymanthus. On his way Heracles stayed for the night with Centaurs on Mount Pholoe; in the evening they held a banquet, and Pholus, the host, brought out wine for his guest, a drink never before tasted by the Centaurs; the moment they smelt it they became intoxicated and began to cause an uproar. Heracles fought with them and they fled to their mountain homes. The banquet was resumed with soft drinks and Heracles sang of his labours; when he reached the story of the Hydra, Pholus asked to see the poisonous arrows, but still a little drunk, he dropped one on his foot and was dead in an instant. Heracles would one day encounter the Centaurs again.

Heracles had no difficulties in trapping the boar, using the same nets with which the Cerynitian Hind had been ensnared. He was beginning to tire of the labours and when he reached Tiryns, entered the city against the orders of Eurystheus, and threatened to throw the monster into the storage jar in which Eurystheus had fled for refuge.

RIGHT Heracles hurls the Erymanthian Boar at Eurystheus; *Athenian black-figure amphora, mid 6th century* BC. *Heracles threatens to put the captured boar into the sunken storage jar where Eurystheus has been hiding.*

V *The Cleansing of the Augeian Stables*

After absconding with Jason and the Argonauts on their quest for the Golden Fleece, Heracles returned to Tiryns for his fifth labour set by Eurystheus, angry at Heracles' recent disappearance. In a single day Heracles was to muck out the stables of the cattle of Augeias, King of Elis in the Peloponnese. Augeias' wealth depended on large herds of cattle, but there were so many of them that their dung lay too thickly on the fields for them to be tilled. Heracles demanded a payment of one-tenth of the cattle, and then proceeded to break a hole in the wall of the enclosure at a weak point shown to him by Athene, who was now his patron deity. He dug channels from the rivers Alpheius and Peneius and the area was flushed clean. Augeias refused to hand over the cattle and Heracles returned enraged to Tiryns where, to add salt to his wound, Eurystheus again refused to count it as a labour since Heracles had demanded a payment.

RIGHT Heracles and Athene cleaning the Augeian Stables; *metope sculpture from the Temple of Zeus at Olympia, c460* BC. *Athene points to a weak spot in the river bank for Heracles to break and flood the land. This was the last of twelve sculpted metopes depicting the Labours; it was placed at the climax because the Labour was local to Olympia. Heracles' hair was left flat for paint and a metal helmet was attached to the holes in Athene's head. Athene's rather heavy drapery and relaxed standing pose are typical of Early Classical art.*

VI *The Stymphalian Birds*

Eurystheus sent Heracles back into Arcadia where a flock of birds, to escape local wolves, had settled on an island in the middle of Lake Stymphalus where they were now creating a nuisance to the local fishermen. The birds were hiding in the rushes when Heracles arrived armed with a pair of bronze castanets forged for him by Hephaestus. He climbed to the top of a mountain overlooking the lake and began to clash the castanets with all his might. Alarmed, the birds took flight in different directions; but Heracles had his catapult at the ready and many of them fell into the lake, others escaping never to return again.

VII *The Cretan Bull*

To date, all of Heracles labours had been in the Peloponnese on mainland Greece; there were no more monsters left for him to kill, no more fabulous creatures to bring home alive, and no more public nuisances to be cleaned up, so now Eurystheus asked his friends overseas if they had any similar problems. King Minos of Crete sent word that there was a wild bull roaming the fields outside of his palace at Knossos. In fact this was the bull that his wife Pasiphae had tricked into making love to her; she had been inspired with lust for the creature by Poseidon when Minos had refused to sacrifice this particularly handsome

bull to the god. Every morning she would go out into the fields and attempt to seduce it, but to no avail – it was more interested in the dewy grass. The great craftsman Daedalus was asked to find a solution, and a few days later he presented her with a hollow wooden cow on wheels, which the next morning was pushed into the bull's field with a rather uncomfortable Pasiphae inside. It had the desired effect and Pasiphae's next baby had the head of a bull and was therefore named the Minotaur (Minos-Bull). Minos and Pasiphae were so embarrassed that they instructed Daedalus to construct the Labyrinth, a vast network of vaults beneath the palace, as a home for their curious son. Perhaps Minos wished to do away with his son's real father, and Heracles was the man to do it. The bull was brought back alive to Eurystheus, and one evening broke its tether and wandered off to Marathon ravaging the countryside until the arrival of Theseus.

VIII *The Mares of Diomedes*

Eurystheus heard that in Thrace there existed four horses, mares owned by the wicked king Diomedes, which lived on human flesh; with any luck they would be hungry when Heracles arrived to capture them for his eighth labour. Heracles made the long journey to Thrace by ship with Abderus, the young lover he had taken after the tragic loss of Hylas. Together they overpowered the grooms, but the alarm was raised and as they rushed the horses down to the waiting ship, Diomedes and his guard came in pursuit; Abderus went ahead with the mares while Heracles turned to kill Diomedes and sent his men running for cover. But when Heracles arrived at the beach he found that the four mares had proved too wild for his young friend and were finishing their tasty meal. Heracles drove them into the ship's hold and returned to bury what remained of Abderus, founding the city of Abdera on the burial mound in his memory. The mares were taken to Tiryns, where Eurystheus freed them; on their way back to Thrace they were attacked by wolves on the slopes of Mount Olympus.

IX *The Belt of Hippolyte*

The next labour turned into a romantic adventure. Eurystheus' daughter Admete had as a child been told stories about the Amazons, a race of female warriors who lived beside the Black Sea on the River Thermodon. In her imagination she developed an admiration for their leader, Queen Hippolyte, who apparently wore a beautiful belt, studded with jewels. Admete suggested that Heracles should fetch it for her, and off he sailed with a crew of heroes. After a number of hostile encounters they arrived at last at Themiscyra, where the queen had her palace. Hippolyte was invited to a banquet on board during which she was struck by the charm of these handsome Greek heroes and wishing to ally herself to them, promised her belt to Heracles. Hera, annoyed at how smoothly Heracles was handling the task, disguised herself as an Amazon and informed the others that their queen was about to be kidnapped. The Amazons immediately attacked the ship and Heracles, thinking that Hippolyte had set him up, killed her and took the belt. Meanwhile, Prince Theseus, one of Heracles' companions, had fallen in love with Antiope, Hippolyte's sister, and he took her with him back to Athens.

X *The Cattle of Geryon*

Heracles delivered the belt to Eurystheus who gave it to his delighted daughter on her next birthday. There were three more labours left and Eurystheus was starting to panic, for he knew full well that if Heracles completed them he would claim his right to the throne at Tiryns. For the tenth labour therefore he decided that a really long journey to bring back the cattle of Geryon, a man with three heads, would exhaust

LEFT Heracles and the Stymphalian Birds; *Athenian black-figure amphora, mid 6th century BC. Heracles uses a catapult to kill the birds, some of which can be seen falling from the sky while others continue to glide gracefully along on the lake. The painter has applied much purple and white to give colour to the exotic birds.*

Heracles and that he would fall easy prey to one of the many monsters encountered on the way: there were plenty of them, for Heracles had never travelled westwards before. Geryon was King of Erytheia (Cadiz), and employed the herdsman Eurytion with his two-headed dog Orthus, son of Typhon, to guard his fine cattle. Heracles enjoyed the outward journey, killing all sorts of beasts on the way, and when he arrived at Oceanus on the edge of the world, he set up a pillar on either side of the straits which divide Africa and Europe as a monument to his great voyage. (They are still there, one now named the Rock of Gibraltar, the other the Jebel Musa in Morocco.) The Pillars of Heracles also served to keep the hideous sea-monsters of Oceanus out of the Mediterranean – they were too large to squeeze through.

Heracles leaned back against one

LEFT Heracles in the bowl of the Sun; Athenian red-figure wine-cup, early 5th century BC. The scene was painted in the bowl of the wine-cup, thus Heracles would appear to be floating in the wine when the cup was full. The sea is denoted by the octopuses and fish.

of the pillars, feeling tired and irritable and extremely thirsty. In his anger at the intense heat of the sun he rashly let loose an arrow in the direction of Helius, charioteer of the Sun. Luckily for him, Helius was in a good mood and admiring the daring of the hero, actually lent him his great golden drinking-cup for his journey to Erytheia, not to drink from, but to sail in. Heracles, club in hand to fend off the sharks, made good progress in the magic cup and soon arrived at Mount Abas where Geryon's cattle were grazing. Eurytion and Orthus ran at him, the hound's two heads barking and snarling; Heracles swung his club killing dog and herdsman with one stroke and quickly made off with the cattle. However Geryon had seen the sun bowl glittering in Oceanus and, troops at the ready, was soon pursuing Heracles. The cattle came to a halt at the River Anthemus, where Heracles turned and shot Geryon with three arrows, one for each head. Heracles decided that the strange boat was drawing too much attention and returned it with thanks to Helius, explaining that the cattle would spoil it.

Thus began his long journey eastwards back to Greece, and as Eurystheus had foreseen this proved to be dangerous, as so many coveted the cattle and lay in ambush for them. In Liguria (southern France) he was attacked and fell to his knees, badly wounded. Zeus came to his rescue by sprinkling rocks around Heracles to shield him; Heracles then hurled them at the retreating Ligurians. (The rocks still lie scattered to the west of Marseilles.)

Heracles then made his way down the west coast of Italy, where unbeknown to him the giant Cacus stole some of the cattle and hid them in his cave, which unfortunately for Cacus stood ahead beside the road (on the future site of Rome). As Heracles drove the noisy herd past the cave, the cattle hidden in the cave answered back revealing their hiding-place. Heracles was furious and killed the giant in a wrestling-bout, to the joy of the local people whose lives Cacus had made a misery. News of Heracles the Hero travelled ahead and everywhere in Italy he was met by joyful crowds, cheering and begging him to dispatch their own local nuisance down to Hades. In the lovely regions beneath the volcanic Mount Vesuvius, he founded a town called Herculaneum in his honour, which was destroyed by a violent volcanic eruption many, many centuries later.

Heracles eventually arrived at the tip of the Italian boot, where Hera caused the finest bull in the herd to break loose and swim the narrow straits to Sicily. Heracles asked the god Hephaestus, who had his forge beneath Mount Etna, to come and look after his cattle and swam off to find the bull. Heracles chased it across the island as far as its westernmost tip where the local king Eryx put it in with his own herds. The king wagered his lands against all of Geryon's cattle in a boxing match with the hero; though Eryx, famous for his boxing skills, put up an entertaining fight, Heracles son of Zeus was simply too powerful and soon Eryx lay dead. Mount Eryx remains as a memorial to the king.

XI *The Apples of the Hesperides*

When Hera married Zeus she had received many fine wedding presents from gods, giants and mortals alike, but her favourite gifts were some golden-apple trees created specially by Gaia, the earth mother. They grew somewhere in the west, but no one knew quite where. Heracles, for his eleventh labour was to bring back the valuable fruit to Eurystheus. Only Nereus, the Old Man of the Sea, knew where they grew and Heracles caught him napping on the sea-shore. Nereus turned himself into all sorts of slippery sea-creatures in an effort to escape, but Heracles' grip was too strong and soon the old man was telling where they could be found. It would not be easy for they were tended by the

Hesperides, Daughters of Evening, who lived near their father where Helius drives his chariot into Oceanus; and the tree on which the apples grew was entwined by a 100-headed snake called Ladon. Heracles had encountered monsters of this type before and did not foresee any difficulties. But, on the way, passing through the Caucasus mountains, he found the Titan, Prometheus, chained to a rock as eternal punishment for deceiving Zeus and stealing fire from the gods to give to men; Zeus' eagle was busy pecking his liver, which was renewed every day. Heracles decided to free the hero and shot the eagle. Prometheus in return advised Heracles to ask Atlas, the Titan whom Zeus had forced to carry the sky, to fetch the apples for him.

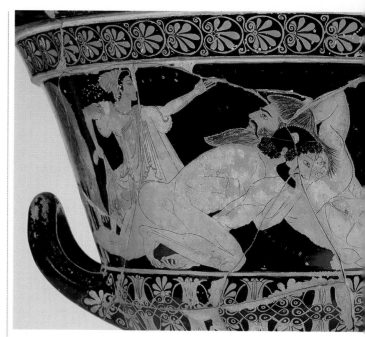

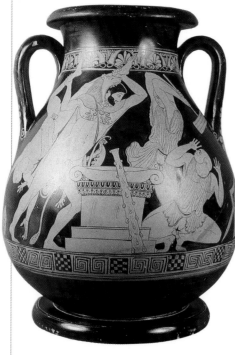

ABOVE Heracles and Busiris; Athenian red-figure pelike (wine-jar) by the Pan Painter, early 5th century BC. The hero is shown flinging King Busiris onto the altar where he himself was about to be sacrificed. The Egyptians are depicted with Negroid features.

Heracles passed through Arabia into Egypt, ruled at that time by the cruel king Busiris. At the start of his reign there had been terrible droughts which had led to famine. Busiris asked a seer from Greece for advice on what was to be done. The seer found that Zeus was angry with Busiris and was demanding the annual sacrifice of a foreigner in return for good harvests.

Busiris was a practical man and the unfortunate seer became the first of a line of foreign visitors to Egypt to be sacrificial victims. Heracles would make a fine sacrifice and he was bound and adorned and dragged to the altar where his father Zeus recognized him. Heracles broke his bonds in fury and proceeded to kill Busiris, together with his son and the priests, laying them on the altar as that year's sacrifice to Zeus.

From Egypt he made his way along the North African coast and came to Libya, where an eccentric young king called Antaeus ruled. Antaeus would challenge heroic visitors to wrestling matches and had never been beaten; and he always fought to the death. Heracles could not resist the challenge but found Antaeus' abilities to be more than he bargained for; everytime he pinned him to the earth to deliver the final blow Antaeus would throw Heracles off with replenished strength. Then he remembered what he had been told about Antaeus' parentage; his mother was Gaia and he was strong only so long as he kept in contact with her. Heracles changed his tactics by holding Antaeus from mother earth as often as he could, draining his strength and eventually killing him with a bear hug.

ABOVE Heracles fights Antaeus; Athenian red-figure calyx crater (wine mixing-bowl) signed by the painter Euphronios, late 6th century BC. The painter has used diluted 'paint' to depict the unkempt hair of the giant, who is in a highly contorted position while the hero's body is firm and true. The giant's right fingers are already limp as he begins to lose the fight.

At last Heracles saw the faint blue line of the Atlas mountains on the western horizon, their white tops gleaming in the evening sun as he approached. Gradually the shape of two huge legs appeared and he greeted Atlas who was holding up the sky on his shoulders. Remembering the advice of Prometheus, Heracles offered to take the load if Atlas would go and fetch the golden apples from the grove of the Hesperides. Atlas was glad to get the weight off his back and obliged by pushing his way past the Daughters of Evening and strangling the hundred necks of Ladon. On his way back to the Atlas mountains, it dawned on him that he need never hold the sky again, and that Heracles could not come after him since he was unable to put down his load. He informed the hero that he felt like a walk and would take the apples to Tiryns himself. Heracles, for the first time in his life unable to use brute force to escape the predicament, had to rely on the few wits he had. He agreed to the proposal, and asked the Titan to hold the sky whilst he made himself more comfortable by placing a pillow on his shoulders. Atlas, who had no wits at all, laid down the apples and took the sky. Heracles took the apples and walked away laughing.

When he reached Tiryns, Eurystheus would not touch the apples, realizing that they were Hera's, so Heracles dedicated them at Athene's temple, since she had helped him to hold the sky. But she did not want them either and returned the sacred apples to the Hesperides.

RIGHT Athene, Heracles and Atlas with the apples of the Hesperides; *metope sculpture from the temple of Zeus at Olympia, c460 BC. The sculptor has depicted the hero supporting the heavens with Athene providing a helping hand; Atlas holds the apples. This was one of twelve metopes depicting the Labours which were positioned above the temple porches, six at each end.*

61

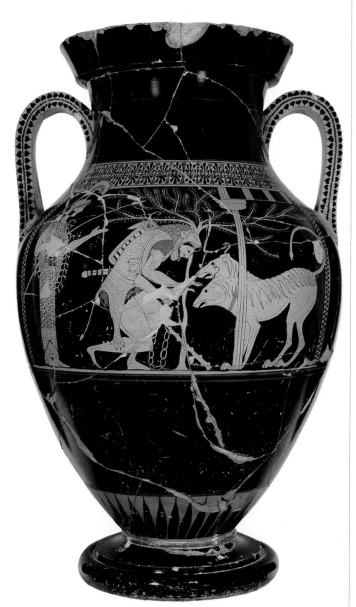

XII *Cerberus*

Eurystheus had to come up with something really lethal for the last labour. There were no more monsters or giants left on the earth; Heracles had annihilated them. 'Why not send him to the Underworld', thought Eurystheus, 'and let us see if he can bring Cerberus, the monstrous hound with three heads and a mane of snakes, up to the land of the living?' Cerberus undoubtedly held a grudge against Heracles for he had killed his brothers and sister: the Nemean Lion, the Hydra, and Orthus the dog.

To prepare himself for this twelfth and most difficult labour, Heracles was required to undergo ritual purification at Eleusis, where he was initiated into the secret Mysteries of Demeter and her daughter Persephone, goddess of the Underworld, to where Heracles now began his journey. Hermes was his guide into Hades' kingdom, and his patron deity Athene went with them as far as the gates near the birdless Lake Avernus. He tricked Cerberus by throwing him a cake soaked in opium, and while the dog snored Heracles pushed his way through the gates into the Underworld. As he became accustomed to the dark, he noticed the ghostly forms of the dead flitting away from him in fear; they appeared to be thirsty and Heracles killed one of the cattle of Hades and offered the blood to the shades as a drink. The cowherd protested and soon Heracles had cracked a couple of his ribs, only stopping when Persephone protested. In the mists he caught sight of two old friends, the heroes Theseus and Peirithous, who were seated in the two Chairs of Forgetfulness, Hades' punishment for attempting to carry off his wife Persephone. The chairs were of cold stone and anyone who sat in them turned to stone and became part of them, like enthroned statues of gods. He freed Theseus, but was afraid to untie Peirithous, the Lapith king, since the ground quaked as he approached him; Peirithous remains there to this day.

LEFT Heracles and Cerberus; Athenian red-figure amphora by the Andokides Painter, late 6th century BC. The hero, holding a chain, approaches the dog with caution; Cerberus here has only two heads, each of which is surmounted by a cobra-like snake. Athene stands close by. The entrance to Hades is depicted as a temple porch.

Hades, seeing the havoc that the heroes were causing, agreed to Heracles' request to take Cerberus to Tiryns, but stipulated that Heracles must try to tame him without weapons, and return him as soon as the people of Tiryns had seen him. Heracles reluctantly agreed; he felt naked without his favourite weapons, but Hades was a god and he dutifully laid down his club, quiver and bow. Again he had to use his brain, and it occurred to him that dogs always attacked people who appeared to be frightened of them; so Heracles walked up casually to Cerberus and, patting him on his three heads, put a chain round each one and took him for a walk to the world above. Cerberus was delighted with this attention and barked with joy all the way to Tiryns. Eurystheus could not believe the advanced warnings of the hound's approach and stood on the ramparts laughing and calling the people of Tiryns to rejoice with him that Heracles was dead; there was a sudden terrifying growl behind him (Heracles had already trained Cerberus to attack cowards) and Eurystheus was back in his jar in a flash of Zeus' thunderbolt. Heracles was about to unchain his new pet, when Eurystheus reminded him that the labours were a sacred purification ceremony and that the gods would be angry if he let Cerberus loose. Heracles reluctantly agreed and took Cerberus back to the gates of Hades.

BELOW Heracles brings Cerberus to Eurystheus; black-figure hydria (water jug), mid 6th century BC. *The hero and king are both painted white, a colour normally reserved for women: perhaps it suggests their terror of the three-headed dog, whom the painter has depicted in black, white and purple with snakes on heads and paws.*

Heracles and Omphale

The twelve labours were over and Heracles remembered the words of the Pythia, who had promised that he would now achieve immortality. But such a promise does not bring happiness on earth, and for the rest of his life Heracles received more than his fair share of human misery. He could never find himself a new wife, since the story of his insane slaughter of Megara and their children was too well known. King Eurytus, who had once taught Heracles archery, refused the hand of his daughter and Heracles took some of his cattle instead. When accused of the theft by Iphitus, son of Eurytus, Heracles threw him off the roof of his palace. The gods punished him with illness; once again he went to Delphi for advice, but the Pythia, considering that he had not grown wiser after the labours, refused to answer him. In his anger he stormed off, taking the sacred tripod of Apollo with him. A fierce fight broke out between him and Apollo for the tripod, Heracles' first encounter with an Olympian; he was doing well and Zeus stopped the fight with a well-aimed thunderbolt and then ordered the Pythia to advise him of his new punishment. He was to be sold into slavery for three years, the proceeds going to the orphans of Iphitus.

At the slave market he was bought at a high price by Omphale, the beautiful Queen of Lydia. He cleared her land of giants and monsters, and some say also served her as a lover. Later authors even suggest that at Omphale's suggestion he wore womens' clothes and took to spinning and playing the lyre. However he spent his time in Lydia, he was still under the orders of the queen and after three years had become healthy again.

Heracles and Deianeira

After years spent avenging himself on former enemies, Heracles went to live in the court of King Oeneus of Calydon. He fell in love with princess Deianeira, but had to

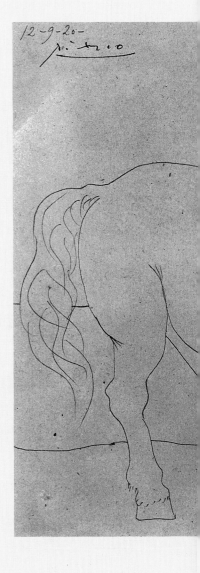

fight the local river-god Achelous for her hand; during the struggle Heracles broke off one of the god's horns which he later presented to the Hesperides, who filled it to the brim with fruit and named it the Cornucopia ('horn of plenty'). Heracles married Deianeira, but they were exiled from Calydon when Heracles, still not knowing his own strength, accidentally killed Oeneus's cup-bearer with a rap on the knuckles for spilling wine at a banquet. They made for Trachis and en route had to cross the wide river Evenus; Heracles was capable of swimming to avoid the high fees of the ferryman, the Centaur Nessus, so he put Deianeira on the ferry whilst he himself swam. In the middle of the river he heard the cries of his wife whom Nessus was trying to rape. Heracles reached the opposite shore and killed the Centaur with an arrow, dipped in the poison of the Hydra. As he lay dying, Nessus, pretending remorse, told Deianeira that she should smear his blood on Heracles' clothes as a magical love potion which would make him always attracted by her. Fearing that one day Heracles would leave her for another woman she bottled the potion for future use.

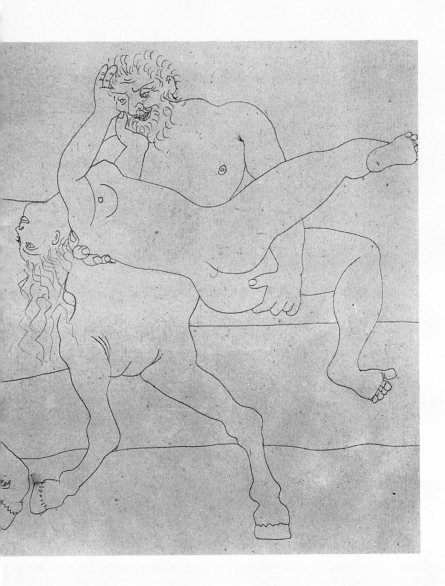

LEFT *Pablo Picasso (1881–1973), Nessus and Dejanira (1920). Picasso carried Classical subjects into the present century. He was particularly interested in figures symbolic of the animal nature of man and made many sketches of the Minotaur. Here he depicts another classic half-man/half-beast, the Centaur Nessus, attempting the rape of Deianeira. The pencil drawing exhibits Picasso's mastery of foreshortening by means of single lines in the manner of Athenian red-figure vase-painters.*

Heracles was welcomed by the people of Trachis and helped them in many battles. He had one last vendetta against King Eurytus of Oechalia, who had once refused him his daughter Iole, as the prize of an archery contest won by Heracles. Eurytus was defeated and on his way back to Trachis with his new concubine Iole, Heracles stopped at Cape Cenaeum on the island of Euboea to build an altar to Zeus. He had no clean clothes for the sacrifice and sent his herald to Trachis to ask Deianeira for a fresh tunic. Deianeira heard from the herald Lichas that Heracles was in love with Iole, and,

remembering the Centaur's advice, smeared the tunic with the love potion. Heracles stood before the altar of Zeus in his new clothes. As he began the sacrifice his flesh began to burn; he ripped off the tunic, which took the flesh with it. In agony, he made his way back to Trachis where he found that Deianeira had committed suicide on learning that she had brought about the death of her husband.

The dying Heracles climbed Mount Oeta with his son Hyllus and ordered him to build a funeral pyre. The hero could not wait to die, but no one could bring themselves to light the pyre. At

last prince Philoctetes, who was passing by with his flocks, agreed to perform the sombre duty; Heracles rewarded him with his bow and arrows. A great crowd had gathered to witness the last moments of the great hero; they watched until the flames began to die away, and just as they were turning to depart a huge cloud rose above the pyre and there was a flash of lightning. The mists dispersed and no sign could be seen of the hero's body. Hyllus recalled the words of the Delphic oracle, related to his father many years earlier, that he would achieve immortality upon completion of the twelve labours.

Heracles was taken to Olympus by Athene and Hermes, where he was introduced to his divine father Zeus for the first time in his immortal life. He was reconciled with Hera, who gave him her daughter Hebe as a wife. Heracles continued to support his worldly allies against Eurystheus, who outlived Heracles on earth as king of Tiryns, and against the Trojans; Philoctetes was persuaded to join the Greeks on the Trojan plain where he killed Paris with the arrows of Heracles. Heracles remained hero of heroes for evermore.

LEFT The introduction of Heracles to Olympus; *Athenian black-figure wine-cup signed by the potter Phrynos, mid 6th century* BC. *This miniature scene was painted on the lip of the wine-cup. Athene, wearing her aegis (breastplate), introduces the hero to his father Zeus. Phrynos epoiesen chairemen ('Phrynos made this and sends his greetings') is signed beneath the scene. It exhibits the fine use of both brush and incising tool by a group of painters known as the 'Little Masters'. On the opposite side of the cup the painter depicted the birth of Athene, emphasizing the brother/sister relationship of goddess and hero.*

Archaeology and Temples

Most Greek myths and legends had geographical locations in the real Greek world and covered the whole of the Mediterranean region. This does not necessarily mean that all Greeks had been to all places mentioned in the myths; the poets might have sometimes intentionally chosen unknown and therefore exotic settings for their stories which would have enhanced the magical and fantastic elements. (Shakespeare, for similar reasons, set many of his plays in real but exotic places where anything could happen.)

Perhaps the most famous location is Mount Olympus, the mythical home of the Olympian gods. Its snowy peaks are rarely visible, often shrouded in clouds which added to the sense of awe felt by the Greeks towards this most sacred of places. Archaeologists have recently discovered a ruined temple on the summit (at 9,186 ft/2,800 m), almost certainly dedicated to Zeus, the king of the Olympian gods. It is unlikely that this inhospitably sited temple was often used for worship, but remains of animal sacrifices, dedicatory inscriptions, and coins have been found in the recent excavations. It was linked by a sacred way to the city of Dion, down in the valley; here there were many rich temples dedicated to various Olympians. A statue of Dionysus, not one of the original twelve Olympians, and a temple of the Egyptian goddess Isis have also been found; the temple of Isis was built during the later Hellenistic period when the Greek world had expanded to embrace alien cultures and their religions. Dion was also the original location of the Olympic Games, organized in honour of Zeus, before they were transferred in the 8th century BC to Olympia in the Peloponnese. One tradition also places the home of the nine Muses, daughters of Zeus and Mnemosyne (Memory), on nearby Mount Pieria.

Other locations included well-known natural features of the landscape: Mount Etna in Sicily (which was full of Greek colonies) was for some the workshop of Hephaestus; others located the divine smith on the island of Lemnos,

ABOVE *Mount Olympus, Greece; the snowy peak is nearly always obscured by clouds.*

which had once been volcanic. Ancient writers of guide-books, such as Pausanias in the 2nd century AD pointed out other peculiar natural features such as boulders and chasms and explained them with myths.

Archaeologists have discovered clues as to the possible origins of certain myths. Romantic 19th-century travellers thought that they had discovered the Labyrinth of the Minotaur at Knossos in Crete; what they actually saw was the many-corridored prehistoric Minoan palace, but even this might have suggested the Labyrinth to the ancient poetic imagination.

Excavations at Troy have uncovered many stages of the ancient city; there is one particularly imposing city (Troy VI) which suffered great devastation in the 13th century BC (dated by pottery); this date approximately accords with the traditional dating of the fall of Troy in the early 12th century BC. It is highly probably that there was a siege of Troy by a confederacy of Greek nations, and that legendary figures like Achilles, Paris and Helen did exist; it would have been quite natural for the epic poets to exaggerate their strength and beauty for the amusement of their audiences. Other 'mythical' features such as monsters and divine epiphanies can be 'explained' in the same manner.

BELOW *Troy and the Trojan plain; the site of Homer's Troy was already a place of pilgrimage in antiquity. Great generals such as Alexander the Great, Julius and Augustus Caesar visited it to pay their respects to the* legendary heroes who had fought and died there. The Greek forces were encamped on the plain beside the sea. The site now bears the trenches and mounds of Schliemann's 19th-century excavations.

BOTTOM *The Trojan walls; these are the remains of later walls and a tower, but they give some idea of the size of the Homeric city, described in the Iliad as 'spacious' and 'surrounded by rings of stone'.*

RIGHT *The Athenian Acropolis ('Top of the City') was the main sanctuary of Classical Athens. It rises steeply from the plain and overlooks the whole of the city. This is a view of the Propylaea (entrance gates) with the little Temple of Athene Nike to the right. On the extreme right appears the top of the Parthenon.*

BELOW *The Parthenon or Temple of Athene Parthenos ('The Virgin') was designed by the architect Ictinus and built between 447 and 432 BC. Its partial survival is due to its conversion into a church and later a mosque. The many decorative sculptures have been destroyed or plundered over the years. Phidias's famous chryselephantine statue of Athene once stood inside.*

The Olympian gods were worshipped in walled sanctuaries. The most important building within the sanctuary was the temple, which was the home of the cult statue of the god; the temple was surrounded with a colonnade and was often decorated with sculptures referring to myths associated with the god (in much the same way as our churches have stained-glass windows illustrating bible stories). Before the temple, which faced the rising sun, was the altar where animal sacrifices were performed by priests or priestesses in front of worshippers who stood under colonnaded shelters called 'stoas'. Around the temple stood votive statues and other offerings dedicated by worshippers. Those who could not afford expensive bronze or marble statues would purchase terracotta images of the gods from booths outside the sanctuary; these were placed on the temple steps and later buried in sacred trenches which are today a rich source for our knowledge of Greek art and religion.

In the larger 'Panhellenic' sanctuaries such as that of Zeus at Olympia and Apollo at Delphi, city states would build their own treasuries along the sacred ways; these were often very fine buildings like miniature temples in which valuable offerings to the god were stored. Athletic competitions would be held every four years in honour of the gods; these sanctuaries therefore also contained stadia, gymnasia and statues of victorious athletes. A truce would be called throughout the Greek world whilst the games were being performed.

BELOW *The Sanctuary of Apollo at Delphi; the site was built on the side of a rocky mountain. In the foreground are the seats of the theatre with the Temple of Apollo behind.*

THESEUS

Aegeus, King of Athens, could not have children and sought the advice of the Delphic oracle. The Pythia's answer was that he should not loosen the spout of his wineskin until he arrived back at Athens. Aegeus did not understand the riddle and went to seek advice from his friend King Pittheus of Troezen before returning home. Pittheus grasped the Oracle's meaning immediately but pretended not to understand as he had hopes for his daughter Aethra; he plied Aegeus with wine and sent Aethra to sleep with him. The following morning the King of Athens left an ivory-handled sword and sandals beneath a huge rock in the palace yard, instructing the princess that if she bore a son who was able to lift the stone, she should send the boy to Athens with the sandals on his feet and the sword at his side. Little did he know that Poseidon came to Aethra on the same night.

The Labours of Theseus

Aethra did have a son and she named him Theseus. He grew into a strong and handsome young man, as might be expected, and believed his grandfather Pittheus who told him that his father was a god. Theseus loved to listen to the travelling poets with their stories of gods, giants and the heroes of Troy; but there was one hero who was still alive

and yet was already the subject of epic tales. His name was Heracles, and Theseus wished that he could one day be the subject of such grand stories. Theseus differed from Heracles in one respect: he was quick-witted and cultured, turning the brutish sport of wrestling into an athletic event for the highly skilled. One day Theseus lifted the stone, which had always been an obstacle to his gymnastic training, and Pittheus told him the story of Aegeus' sword and sandals. Theseus decided to set out for Athens, but refused to take the short sea crossing across the Saronic Gulf, preferring to travel on foot across the Isthmus which joins the Peloponnese to Attica. His excuse was that he suffered from sea-sickness, but really he wanted a chance to encounter the monsters and giants who, it was rumoured, lived beside this well-trodden route.

All travellers from southern to northern Greece were compelled to cross the narrow Isthmus; therefore, not surprisingly, many robbers dwelt in the area and made a living as highwaymen. One of the most notorious and feared was the giant Sinis, known as Pityocamptes; this name meant 'Pine-Bender' and referred to the manner in which Sinis would slay his victims. He used two methods: in one he would help the traveller to bend the top of a pine to the ground, at the last moment letting go so that the unwary stranger was shot high into the air; the second method was more terrible, Sinis would attach the victim's legs one to each of two bent pines and then release the trees, tearing the stranger in two. Theseus dispatched Sinis by the second method.

On his journey to Athens, Theseus also discovereed wild beasts and monsters which had been left alone by Heracles. One of these was a huge sow called Phaea by her parents Typhon and Echidna, children of Titans; the beast was terrorizing the farms around Crommyon, but Theseus killed her with a single blow. Already Theseus was becoming renowned in Greece, and it was not long before rumours of this new hero had reached King Aegeus at Athens.

Beside the Isthmus are rocks and cliffs known as the Rocks of Sciron. Passing travellers would be welcomed by Sciron, offered a drink and told to put their feet up. After this refreshment he would ask them to wash his feet in return; but while they were drying his feet he would suddenly kick them unsuspecting over the precipice to fall into the jaws of a giant turtle waiting at the foot of the cliffs. Theseus accepted the hospitality, and returned the favour by washing Sciron's feet, considering this good behaviour for a royal prince. He was too skilled in the art of wrestling for the sudden kick to catch him off his guard and, taking hold of the robber's ankles, hurled him over his shoulders to become the turtle's last meal.

Theseus continued on his way to Athens and soon had reached Eleusis. Here he was welcomed by King Cercyon, who demanded a wrestling bout with the stranger. The king's style of fighting was barbaric and he had already killed a number of passing travellers by sheer brute force. In the palace at Troezen, Theseus had received a fine education in both fighting and the arts, and had developed rules and skills for the generally violent physical activities hoping to encourage sportsmanship among otherwise cultured peoples. Here at Eleusis was his chance to set an example; barbaric Cercyon smashed and grabbed, but Theseus used his skills and swift footwork to avoid and parry the blows, to the delight and applause of onlookers. Cercyon died of sheer exhaustion. Theseus set up a training school at Eleusis where athletes would be taught to box and wrestle in a civilized manner.

Theseus stayed the night just outside Eleusis at the inn of Damastes, whose nickname Procrustes ('Stretcher') was only understood when he showed his guests to their bedrooms. Wanting the tall ones to be comfortable, he made sure that their beds fitted exactly by sawing off any limbs

LEFT The Labours of Theseus; Athenian red-figure wine-cup, 5th century BC. In the centre Theseus kills the Minotaur and pulls the body outside the Labyrinth. Around the outside of the cup the hero punishes Sinis (tied to the tree), Sciron (note the turtle) and Procrustes (having his legs removed to fit the bed) and captures the Bull of Marathon.

which hung over the end of the bed. The short guests would have weights attached to their feet until they also fitted their beds exactly. Theseus put an end to the innkeeper's mad tricks by returning his gruesome hospitality.

On the following morning Theseus at last received his first glimpse of his destination; the palace and shrines on the Acropolis, the precipitous limestone hill which dominates the Athenian plain, were grander than any he had seen. As he was passing by the wayside Temple of Apollo Delphinius, some workmen on the roof of the temple jeered and whistled, thinking from his appearance that he was a young girl. Theseus was always well dressed as a civilized prince should be but he realised that his ankle-length gown was the fashion for Athenian women and that men wore a short tunic. However, he lost his temper and hurled two oxen from a passing cart up above the roof of the temple to the astonishment of the workmen.

King Aegeus had stopped at Corinth on his way back to Athens from Troezen; at the royal palace he had met the oriental princess Medea, who had been spurned by her husband Jason when he took a new wife at Corinth. Medea, famous for her witchcraft, had avenged herself on Jason by killing his new bride with a burning cloak, as well as murdering her two sons by him. She had flown to Athens in a dragon-drawn chariot, the gift of her grandfather Helius, and promised to bear Aegeus children if he would protect her at Athens. They had a son called Medus, whom Medea wished to see made king of Athens. Only she recognized Theseus as the boy whom Aegeus had once told her would one day come to Athens as the royal heir, but she kept this knowledge to herself. Aegeus held a splendid banquet for the new hero, whose exploits along the road from Troezen were already the subject of Athenian drinking songs; Theseus had become as renowned a hero as Heracles.

Medea, however, persuaded Aegeus that Theseus was actually an enemy who had come to overthrow the king; they sent him off to kill the bull of Marathon, which Heracles had brought from Crete years earlier as one of his labours. Medea and Aegeus knew that Theseus would be killed, and that being a hero he could not refuse the challenge. Theseus captured the bull on the plains of Marathon and triumphantly brought it back alive to prove his heroism to the people of Athens; he presented it to Aegeus for sacrifice. That evening at a celebratory banquet Medea slipped poison in the hero's cup; just as he was about to drink, Aegeus noticed the ivory-handled sword hanging at Theseus's side and knocked the poisoned cup from his hands. Theseus was welcomed as the new prince of Athens and the people rejoiced that such a brave and handsome hero would one day be king.

Theseus and the Minotaur

Later that year Theseus learnt of a disturbing event that took place every nine years at Athens. A generation earlier King Minos of Crete had attacked Athens and demanded tribute of seven boys and seven girls, who were to be sent to Crete as a nine-yearly feast for the Minotaur, his monstrous son born from the union of his queen, Pasiphae, and the bull of Marathon when it had lived on Crete; it had a bull's head and a man's body and represented to the Athenians all the uncontrolled lusts and animal qualities of uncivilized barbarians. Theseus asked Aegeus why his own name was not placed in the jar for the lottery which decided which unlucky children were to be sent to Crete; Aegeus laughed and answered that a prince did not count as a tribute. Theseus demanded that he should replace one of the chosen boys – he determined to slay the Minotaur.

The seven boys and seven girls of Athens sailed out from Piraeus, the port of Athens, in the black-sailed ship of Minos himself. Aegeus sadly told the captain to hoist a white sail on the return trip if Theseus was

RIGHT *Theseus and Athene in the underwater palace of Amphitrite; Athenian red-figure wine-cup, signed by Euphronios as potter and Onesimos as painter; early 5th century* BC. *The underwater scene with swimming dolphins and a Triton supporting Theseus' feet would have been enhanced by the sea of wine that covered it. The drapery is depicted swaying in the sea-currents. Euphronios epoiesen ('Euphronios made this') is signed to the left of the young Theseus. On the cup exterior were painted further heroic exploits of Theseus.*

successful, so that preparations could be made for the triumphant home-coming. On the sea-journey to Crete Theseus, hearing the cries of one of the seven girls whom the lusty Minos was pestering, challenged him to a show of strength. Minos called on his father Zeus to hurl a thunderbolt into the sea as proof of his own divine parentage; a flash of lightning duly appeared, and Minos arrogantly threw his gold ring into the sea, challenging Theseus to prove that his father was Poseidon by retrieving it. Theseus dived without hesitation and had soon reached his father's palace; he was welcomed by Amphitrite, the lovely wife of Poseidon, who not only handed him Minos's ring, but also placed on his brow a beautiful wreath of roses and wrapped him in a purple cloak. Theseus was soon standing on deck miraculously dry. The Nereids rode the waves beside the ship and the Athenian children joined them in their songs of praise; Minos was greatly disturbed and left the girls alone for the rest of the journey.

LEFT Theseus fighting the Minotaur; *Athenian red-figure stamnos (wine mixing-jar) by the Kleophrades Painter, early 5th century BC. The hero's pony-tailed hair reflects the new 5th-century fashion for short or tied hair. Diluted 'paint' depicts blood on the Minotaur, who holds a stone as a weapon. Theseus' hat and scabbard hang on the wall.*

RIGHT Theseus and the Minotaur; *Roman wall-painting from a Pompeian house, 1st century AD. The Minotaur lies dead in the entrance to the Labyrinth. The hero is praised by both children and adults.*

RIGHT Dionysus and Ariadne; *red-figure wine-cup, 5th century BC. The drunken Dionysus, wearing an ivy wreath, holds a lyre and is supported by his mortal lover Ariadne. Eros, depicted in the 5th century BC as an adolescent youth with long hair and wings, plays a tambourine. The vine leaves and grapes which decorate the top of the bowl would be reflected in the wine.*

On Crete, as was the custom on the night before feeding them to the Minotaur, Minos entertained his young guests at his palace at Knossos. At the banquet Princess Ariadne fell in love with Theseus and offered to help if he took her back to Athens with him. The Minotaur lived in a maze beneath the palace called the Labyrinth; Ariadne gave Theseus a plan of the Labyrinth which its architect, the famous craftsman Daedalus, had given her to spite King Minos. The next morning the young Athenians were thrown into the maze; Ariadne gave Theseus a ball of string and attached one end of it to the Labyrinth's exit. Theseus stepped into the darkness, unravelling the twine as he stepped over the skeletons of earlier victims. He heard the bellowings of the monster in the distance and made his way towards them; at last he found the Minotaur in a great hall at the centre of the maze about to strangle one of the children. Theseus used his wrestling skills, but finding that they were ineffective against the beast, killed it with a well-aimed blow of his fist. He gathered the Athenians together and, guided by the twine, was soon back in the open air. Ariadne had prepared the ship for sailing and soon they were safely on their way towards Athens. There was great rejoicing on board that night.

The ship stopped for water at the island of Dia (Naxos); where Theseus cruelly abandoned Ariadne on the beach. She watched his ship disappear over the horizon and, greatly distressed, prepared to hang herself; but as she placed the noose around her neck she heard distant music and singing. Coming towards her along the beach was a group of Maenads following a beautiful youth with ivy-strewn hair and a thyrsos in his hand. She knew immediately that this was the god Dionysus and their love lasted for many years. When she died Dionysus placed among the stars the crown which he had given her at their wedding, the constellation Corona Borealis.

Perhaps Theseus' callous behaviour was repaid: as the ship approached Athens, the captain, caught up in the excitement of the rejoicing passengers, had forgotten to hoist the white sail. King Aegeus was standing on the edge of the Acropolis when he saw the mournful sign of the black sail; thinking his son dead, he jumped to his death.

Theseus, King of Athens

Theseus, after mourning his father, received a splendid coronation and set about improving the kingdom of Athens. He persuaded the outlying towns of Athens, the Demes, to support an Athenian commonwealth, and reduced his own royal powers; an early step towards democracy, which later took him as its hero.

Heracles honoured the new king by inviting him on an expedition, his ninth labour, to the Black Sea where the Amazons lived; his task was to bring back the belt of Queen Hippolyte as a gift for Eurystheus' daughter. Hippolyte and her relatives were invited to a banquet on board the Greek ship; Theseus fell in love with Antiope, sister to the queen, and took her back to Athens where they married and had a son called Hippolytus. Antiope was killed when an army of Amazons marched against Athens in an unsuccessful attempt to win her back.

Theseus thought it would be sensible to form a political alliance with Crete and arranged to marry Minos's daughter Phaedra – the abandonment of her sister Ariadne had apparently been forgotten. Demophon and Acamas were their two sons and became heirs to the Athenian throne; Hippolytus had already been sent to Troezen where he became heir to his great-grandfather Pittheus.

During an attempted political coup, Pallas, the half-brother of Aegeus, and his fifty sons were killed by Theseus; the oracle instructed Theseus to go into exile for one year as purification for the spilling of family blood. He decided to spend the year at Troezen. Theseus and his court were welcomed at Troezen by Hippolytus. When Phaedra saw him she shuddered as she recognized the beautiful young man she had once seen at an initiation ceremony to the goddess Demeter at Eleusis. Phaedra's love for this handsome stranger had been inspired by Aphrodite and Phaedra had built a shrine to the goddess on the corner of the Acropolis; on a clear day she could see Troezen, where she knew he lived, but until the day she arrived there with her husband she was unaware that this was the son of Theseus by another woman. Hippolytus himself had become a fine hunter and had vowed his chastity to the virgin goddess of the chase, Artemis.

BELOW *Peter Paul Rubens (1577–1640),* Battle of the Amazons. *Rubens represents a scene popular in Classical art: Greek males fighting the Amazon warriors. The Greeks used the subject to demonstrate the triumph of civilized patriarchal society over barbarian societies with feminine characteristics. The wives of Greek citizens lived in purdah.*

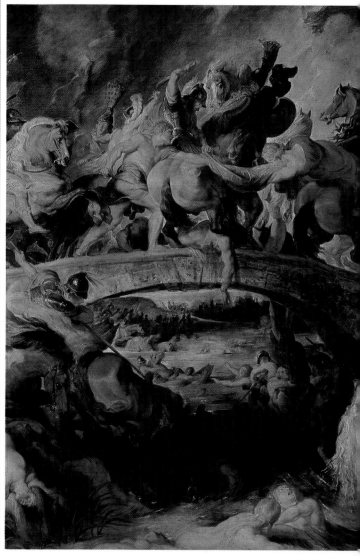

Pierre-Auguste Renoir (1841–1919), Diana (1867). Renoir has painted the virgin Artemis (Diana) as a contemporary beauty seated in a sunny French landscape. She wields a very unclassical longbow with which she has just killed a deer.

While Theseus was away at Delphi Phaedra found herself wasting away with unrequited love for her stepson. Her nurse secretly informed Hippolytus of Phaedra's feelings, but he was disgusted. Phaedra, driven to despair, committed suicide after writing a letter in which she spitefully informed Theseus that Hippolytus had raped her. Theseus returned and read the letter; refusing to believe his son's innocence, he called on his father Poseidon to destroy him. One day Hippolytus was riding his chariot along the beach when a huge bull rose from the sea and terrified the prince's horses; Hippolytus became entangled in the reins and was dragged over the rocks to his death. Theseus later learnt the truth from the priestess of Artemis; Aphrodite had arranged the tragedy because Hippolytus had refused to worship her, preferring chaste Artemis.

The Lapith King Peirithous invited Theseus to his marriage with Hippodameia. He also invited the Centaurs, who have the upper half of men but from the waist downwards are all horse. These semi-wild creatures had never drunk wine before and at the first taste their animal natures took control and they tried to rape the women. A fight ensued between Lapith and Centaur, and, with Theseus leading them, the Lapiths won.

After the deaths of Hippodameia and Phaedra, Peirithous and Theseus decided that they must find divine wives. Theseus forcibly abducted Helen, born from the egg of Zeus after he made love to Leda as a swan; but her heroic brothers, the Dioscuri, Castor and Polydeuces, won her back only to find her abducted again by Paris of Troy. Perithous decided to try to win Persephone from Hades; the two heroes were captured and imprisoned on the two chairs of Lethe (Forgetfulness), to make them forget their sacrilegious act. Heracles freed Theseus when he came on his last labour to capture the guard dog Cerberus.

Theseus, unlike Heracles, died an ignominious mortal death. He slipped over a cliff on the island of Scyros, where he had come to reclaim some lands which had once belonged to his grandfather; some say he was pushed. As he fell towards the rocks below, Theseus remembered the similar fates of the robber Sciron, of his beloved father Aegeus, and of his son Hippolytus.

LEFT Lapith fighting Centaur; metope sculpture from the Parthenon, Athens, 447–432 BC. The Parthenon's exterior Doric frieze was decorated with 92 sculpted metopes. Four subjects were represented, one for each side of the temple: Greeks fighting Trojans; Greeks fighting Amazons; gods fighting giants and Lapiths fighting Centaurs. The subjects symbolized the victory of the civilized Greeks over the Persians earlier in the century. Here the sculptor produces a circular tension between the man and half-beast, while the spread drapery makes an effective backdrop.

BELOW Theseus and Peirithous in the Underworld; Athenian red-figure calyx-crater (wine-mixing jar) by the Niobid Painter, mid 5th century BC. The subject is disputed, but might well depict the two heroes seated in Hades with Heracles and Athene standing above them. The painter has attempted (for the first time in vase-painting) to convey an impression of depth by placing the figures on different levels; the rocky landscape is drawn in thin white lines.

PERSEUS

Acrisius, the King of Argos, had been told by an oracle that he would one day be killed by a grandson. Therefore, he arranged for his daughter Danae to be locked in a cell of bronze until she was too old to have children; one day however he learnt that she had become miraculously pregnant. Zeus had plans for the future of Argos and had come to her one night through an air vent in the roof of the cell as a beautiful shower of gold dust. She bore a son and named him Perseus, but Acrisius had them thrown into the sea in a wooden chest. They were washed up on the island of Seriphos, where a friendly fisherman named Dictys gave them shelter. When Perseus reached manhood, Danae told him who his father was.

Perseus and Medusa

Dictys' lusty brother Polydectes was the King of Seriphos. He wanted to marry Danae but Perseus defended his unwilling mother. Angry at this rebuttal, Polydectes demanded horses from all the islanders as a gift to Hippodameia, daughter of King Oenomaus of Pisa, whom he now wished to marry. Perseus had no horses but said that he would provide anything else that the king might suggest, even the head of the Gorgon Medusa. Polydectes knew that no man had ever returned from visiting the Gorgons and confidently sent Perseus off to fulfil his rash promise.

Zeus sent Athene to give help and advice to his son. She directed him to a cave in Libya, where three hags called the Graeae dwelt; they would tell him where to find certain nymphs who were preparing special weapons to defeat the Gorgons. The Graeae, sisters of the Gorgons, refused to help Perseus. They possessed only one eye and one tooth between them and as one was passing the eye to the other

LEFT *Titian (c1487–1576), Danae and the Shower of Gold, (1554). The painting was commissioned as one of a number of erotic Classical subjects for Philip II of Spain. The painting depicts Danae not in the bronze prison of the Classical myth but in a luxurious bedroom complete with pet dog and a servant who tries to gather the gold in her apron. Titian described the painting as 'poesie' – a poetic fantasy of the myth.*

to look at the stranger, Perseus grabbed it and refused to return it unless they told him the whereabouts of the nymphs. He found them and they presented him with the weapons: a pouch in which to place Medusa's severed head; a pair of winged sandals to make a quick escape from her two immortal sisters, Stheno and Euryale, who had golden wings and hands of bronze; and a magical cap to make him invisible to perform the task. Hermes provided a sickle of sharpened adamant and helped him to polish his bronze shield until it shone like a mirror; this would be useful in enabling him to look at the reflected image of the Gorgons, who turned all who looked at them to stone.

Perseus recognized the approach to the Gorgons' lair by the petrified images of men and women who had caught sight of them; the sisters had placed them like marble statues on either side of the path. Invisible in his magic cap, Perseus approached Medusa, watching her reflection carefully in his shield. She was hideous, with snakes instead of hair and a huge red tongue hanging from her mouth between tusks. Perseus decapitated her with one swing of the sickle and, placing the head in the pouch, flew away swiftly in his winged sandals; Stheno and Euryale could not keep up with him and finally returned to mourn their dead sister.

On the way home Perseus stopped for the night in the land of the Hesperides. Atlas, who stood guard over their garden which contained the magic apples of Hera, had been told that one day a son of Zeus would come and steal them. He therefore tried to kill Perseus, who produced the Gorgon's head and turned the Titan into a high peak, Mount Atlas.

Perseus and Andromeda

As Perseus flew along the coast of Ethiopia he spied far below a naked girl chained to a rock by the sea. He flew nearer and heard her crying for help; two sad figures, her parents King Cepheus and Queen Cassiopeia, were standing on the cliff and Perseus learnt from them what was happening: Cassiopeia had vainly boasted that her daughter was prettier than the Nereids; they had complained to Poseidon who had sent a sea-monster to terrorize Ethiopia. An oracle had told Cepheus that the monster would leave them alone only if he were to offer it his daughter Andromeda. Perseus promised to destroy the monster if the king and queen would allow him to marry Andromeda; at that moment the creature raised its long neck above the waves and dived, heading underwater for Andromeda's rock. Cepheus agreed and Perseus slew the monster with his sickle; it lay dead on the beach beneath the lovely Andromeda whom he unchained and delivered back to her parents. There was a celebratory banquet at the palace that night and Cepheus announced his daughter's marriage to the new hero, forgetting that he had already promised her to his brother Phineus. A fight started and Perseus, realizing that he was far outnumbered by Phineus and his troops, petrified them with the head of Medusa.

Perseus sailed to Seriphos with

RIGHT: Perseus and the Gorgon Medusa; Athenian black-figure olpe (wine-jug) by the Amasis Painter, mid 5th century BC. Medusa is depicted with fangs, sticking-out tongue and snake-locks. The hero averts his head as he decapitates Medusa so as not to be turned to stone by her gaze. Hermes stands watching. Amasis m'epoiesen ('Amasis made me') is signed to the left of Theseus.

LEFT *Perseus and Medusa; limestone metope sculpture from a Greek temple at Selinus, Sicily, mid 6th century BC. The winged horse Pegasus appears beside his mother Medusa, while Athene stands to the left. The profile bodies with frontal 'smiling' faces are typical of Archaic art.*

Andromeda and discovered on arrival that King Polydectes was still pursuing his mother Danae. Leaving Danae and Andromeda with Dictys, he went to the royal court and announced that he had returned with the gift for Hippodameia; out of its pouch came Medusa's head and all were turned to stone. He returned the magic cap, winged sandals and sickle to Hermes who took them back to the African nymphs; the head of Medusa was dedicated to Athene, who attached it to her aegis (breastplate) as a formidable weapon. Perseus decided to return to his birthplace at Argos and claim his inheritance from King Acrisius.

Though Perseus was prepared to forgive his past behaviour, Acrisius fled to King Teutamides, remembering the prophetic words of the oracle. Perseus left Danae and Andromeda at Argos and travelled to Larisa, where Teutamides was holding funeral games in honour of his father. Perseus could not see Acrisius among the crowds of spectators and decided to wait until the evening banquet; in the meantime he would compete in the games and introduced an event of his own called 'throwing the discus'. He took up the metal disk and hurled it into the open spaces of the stadium; but the wind suddenly diverted it and the discus landed in the crowd, killing Acrisius and thus fulfilling the prophecy.

Perseus returned to his mother and wife at Argos, but realized that the gods would consider it wrong for him to rule over the city of the man he had killed. He therefore exchanged Argos with nearby Tiryns where he ruled for many years, founding several other cities in the Argolid including Mycenae. Andromeda bore him several children and his grandson Eurystheus became the last of the Perseid dynasty at Argos. Perseus died a natural death.

LEFT *Sir Edward Coley Burne-Jones (1833–98), The Doom Fulfilled. Burne-Jones brings a Romantic medieval atmosphere to the myth of Perseus' rescue of Princess Andromeda. The hero's armour and winged greaves are distinctly exotic whilst the hair of Medusa's head spills from his shoulder-bag. Andromeda is free of her chains but awaits the outcome of the fight.*

The Greek Poets

RIGHT Rhapsode reciting; *Athenian red-figure amphora by the Kleophrades Painter, early 5th century* BC. *The painter has inscribed the start of an epic poem emerging from the poet's mouth: 'As once in Tiryns . . .'. Tiryns was a powerful Greek Mycenaean palace at the time of the Trojan war.*

In prehistoric Greece the myths were transmitted orally by professional poets called 'rhapsodes'. Their patrons were the Greek-speaking kings and aristocrats who governed relatively small areas of the Mediterranean. The rhapsodes would travel from court to court, often staying for several days to recite lengthy epic poems from memory: Mnemosyne (Memory) was the mother of the Muses who inspired poets. These epics were first recorded by poets such as Homer when writing was introduced in the 8th century BC. Their subjects concerned the origins of the gods and giants as well as legends of wars fought by their ancestors centuries ago. The most popular saga was the siege of Troy by the Greeks and their heroic adventures both before and after the siege. Relying on memory and wishing to hold the attention of their audiences, who would normally be wining and dining, the rhapsodes decorated their stories with superhuman activities and encounters with gods and monsters. Their language was suitably high-flown and the poems were sung in strict metre often to musical accompaniment.

Here is a description of the Greek hero Achilles from Homer's *Iliad*, translated by Alexander Pope in 1715:

> The Hero rose;
> Her aegis Pallas o'er his shoulders throws;
> Around his brows a golden cloud she spread;
> A stream of glory flamed above his head.
> As when from some beleaguered town arise
> The smokes high-curling to the shaded skies
> (seen from some island, o'er the main afar,
> When men distressed hang out the sign of war),
> Soon as the Sun in ocean hides his rays,
> Thick on the hills the flaming beacons ablaze;
> With long-projected beams the seas are bright,
> And heaven's high arch reflects the ruddy light;
> So from Achilles' head the splendours rise,
> Reflecting blaze on blaze against the skies.

There were also the lyric poets, who composed short poems for the symposia, intimate drinking parties held among a few close friends; they sung in short verses and accompanied themselves on the lyre – hence the name 'lyric'. Their subject matter was more personal than epic, dealing with apparently spontaneous outpourings of love, political satire and other themes relating to the lie of the *polis* (city-state). One of the earliest surviving lyric poets is

Sappho of Lesbos (c620–c550 BC), who recited her poems at symposia which seem to have been attended mainly by women.

In the following poem Sappho employs the myth of Helen to show the power of Aphrodite in influencing feelings of love. Sappho subverts the male values of war, preferring unadorned natural female beauty to the artificial glamour of armed warriors.

What is the most beautiful sight on this black earth?
Some will answer cavalry, or infantry, or warships;
But the woman I most love
Is lovelier than all these.

My answer is easily explained,
For Helen, more beautiful than all on earth,
Left doting parents, princely husband, child
To cross the sea for Troy: love at first sight.

After all, teenage brides have fragile hearts,
Which filled with passions newly poured
Are readily persuaded
By Aphrodite, Cypriot Queen.

I am no different when I think of Anaktoria
As she left me: at her sensual walk and glimmering
    pearly face
I would prefer to gaze
than richly decorated Lydian chariots filled with
    weapons.

(Translated by David Bellingham)

Choral odes were composed by lyric poets for more public occasions, such as weddings and religious festivals. These would include a colourful mixture of song and dance delivered by a chorus. They would employ myths to honour the patron, which might be a newly wed couple, a victor in the athletic games, or the *polis* itself. Bacchylides, writing in the 5th century BC, composed a choral hymn of praise to the hero Theseus, to be performed at a festival in honour of Apollo on his sacred island of Delos; it was sung by the poet's fellow islanders from Keos. King Minos of Crete, who is bringing Theseus and other young Athenian to offer as a sacrifice to the Minotaur, sends Theseus into the sea to fetch a golden ring to prove his heroism and divine favour. At the end of the poem Theseus emerges

ABOVE Symposium and Gorgon's head; Athenian black-figure wine-cup, mid 6th century BC. *The drinkers hold similar wine-cups and one of them plays the aulos (double-pipe); a naked boy offers more wine. The Gorgon's head would appear as the drinker finished his wine.*

from the sea triumphantly wearing a wreath given to him by the sea-goddess Amphitrite; the mythical narrative ends with songs of praise which return us to the present moment and the festival of Apollo:

> He came to the surface beside the narrow ship's stern;
> What a shock for the King of the armies of Knossos,
> To see him standing there all dry.
> All were amazed at the gleaming godly gifts he wore
> And Nereids cried in delight from their glittering
>   thrones
> Riding the sea which echoed with their laughter.
> The young Athenians praised him with songs of love.
> Lord of Delos, your soul moved by our Kean voices,
> Now send us your blessings from the heavens above.

(Trans. David Bellingham)

In the 5th century BC Athens was at the centre of Greek culture, attracting the best artists and writers with wealthy patronage. The most influential poetic form at this time was tragedy. Annual festivals to Dionysus culminated in dramatic competitions in the large open-air theatre of Dionysus on the slopes of the Acropolis. These plays took the form of trilogies performed in one day with a 'satyr play' in the evening to lighten the mood. Their subjects were drawn from mythology, but they usually dealt with matters of contemporary relevance: in the *Oresteia* trilogy by Aeschylus we are taken from the aftermath of the Trojan wars in the first two plays to contemporary Athens in the final play where we witness the first trial by jury under the new democracy. Other plays, such as Euripides' *Trojan Women* (415 BC), deal with Greek attitudes towards women; Andromache speaks:

> The woman whom people really gossip about
> Is the one who refuses to remain housebound.
> I would love to have gone out, but dutifully
> Stayed at home; and I did not answer back
> Like some women do. My mind was sound enough
> And taught me how to behave as nature intended.
> What more did I need?
> I would speak only when spoken to
> And appear meek and mild before my husband.
> I knew what was expected of me
> And when to let him have his own way.

(Translated by David Bellingham)

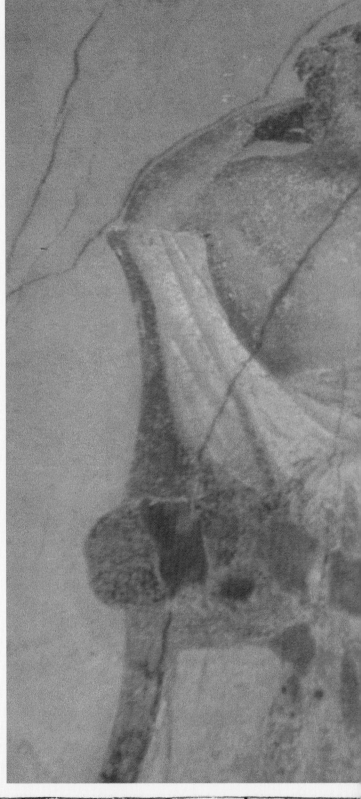

These early poetic uses of myth continued into the Hellenistic and Roman periods, but there are changes of emphasis. Greek poetry and art continued to be signs of high cultural attainment for Hellenistic kings and Roman emperors. Poets became increasingly learned in their use of myth and expected similar levels of understanding in their audiences. Callimachos, librarian at Alexandria in Egypt in the 3rd century BC, wrote for a royal patron and his court. An increasing tendency among poets in the Hellenistic period was to dwell on the minor details and previously unimportant episodes of the myths: the heroes and heroines became more human and Callimachos responded to a desire among the sophisticated urban elite for romantic images of country peasants. In the poem 'Hecale', Theseus is on his way to fight the bull of Marathon and seeks shelter from a storm in an old woman's cottage:

Theseus threw off his soaking clothes
And putting on a ragged tunic that she had laid out on
    the bed
Made himself at home on her humble couch.
She meanwhile had built a fire from wood stored long
    ago
And brought him a cauldron of boiling water;
'Have you a bowl for me to soak my feet in?', asked
    Theseus.
When he had finished she emptied the bowl and brought
    him
Another cup of wine and water.
She brought him black and green olives, which she had
    gathered wild
In the Autumn, now swimming in brine;
From a pipkin she served him loaves,
And while Theseus ate the ploughman's lunch,
Hecale told him the story of her life
For she had once come from a wealthy family . . .

(Translated by David Bellingham)

LEFT The poet Menander; *Roman wall-painting from the House of the Menander, Pompeii, 1st century* AD. *Menander was a 4th-century* BC *writer of Greek comedy. He is shown here reading from a papyrus scroll, the normal medium for published poetry.*

FOUR

Tales of Gods, Heroes & Mortals

This chapter relates a number of short stories of various types, culled from many sources. They have been subdivided into 'Encounters with Monsters', 'Tales of Tragic Romance', 'Stories of Metamorphosis' and 'Stories of Divine Retribution'. As can be seen, the selected demarcations often overlap within a tale.

ENCOUNTERS WITH MONSTERS

Odysseus

Odysseus, King of the island of Ithaca, was one of the great Greek heroes who fought in the siege of Troy. On the return sea-journey he ran into storms caused by the gods, who were angry at the atrocities committed by the Greeks during the sack of Troy. Odysseus and his crew had many adventures before they reached their homes.

On one occasion Odysseus found himself near Sicily and went ashore with a few men to explore. They found a cave filled with food and wine and were about to take this booty back to the ship whey they heard giant footsteps approaching the cave. It was the Cyclopes Polyphemus, one of a race of giant shepherds who had just one eye in the centre of their heads. He entered the cave with his sheep and rolled a huge stone across the entrance. Odysseus expected the normal Greek hospitality, but the barbaric giant replied by eating two of the crew; this practice continued for several days, until cunning Odysseus thought up a plan. They offered Polyphemus some excellent wine which they had brought with them from Greece; he was soon intoxicated and the Greeks heated a pointed stake in the fire and thrust it into the single eye of the giant.

LEFT Polyphemus blinded by Odysseus and friends; *Athenian amphora found at Eleusis, c650 BC. The painting is a very early form of black-figure, with the painter experimenting with sketchy outlines for the figure of Odysseus. Polyphemus' intoxication is indicated by his wine-cup. The triangular torsos and profile legs and heads with frontal eyes are typical of Archaic art.*

91

Next morning the blind Cyclopes felt with his hands every sheep that went out of the cave and counted them in again in the evening, so as not to allow Odysseus and his men their escape. Odysseus thought up another clever plan. The following morning, Polyphemus counted the sheep out of the cave, feeling them carefully to check that they were not human, and rolled the stone across the entrance. Odysseus and his friends had tied themselves to the bellies of the sheep and thus escaped the blind giant's notice. They ran down to the ships and as soon as they were some distance from the shore, Odysseus foolishly began to shout insults at Polyphemus. The infuriated Cyclopes started to hurl boulders at random into the sea and the Greeks were lucky to escape; Polyphemus prayed to his father Poseidon to make trouble for the Greek sailors on their journey home.

After several other adventures the Greeks arrived at the island of Aiaia, off the west coast of Italy. Here lived Circe, lovely daughter of Helius and an Oceanid called Perseis, who was renowned for her knowledge of magical herbs and poisons. Odysseus, not wishing to stray too far from the ships after previous encounters with island monsters, sent scouts ahead to explore. They came to a house in the middle of the woods and were greeted by curiously well-behaved wolves and lions, who invited them to meet their mistress. Circe handed them drugged wine which turned them into pigs. One of the more cautious Greeks had stayed hidden in the bushes and he now returned to Odysseus and the others to tell them what marvels he had witnessed. Odysseus decided to investigate and on his way through the woods, Hermes, in the guise of a handsome youth, met him and offered him a spe-

RIGHT Odysseus and the Sirens; *Athenian red-figure* stamnos *(wine-mixing jar) by the Siren Painter; early 5th century* BC. *Odysseus is shown tied to the mast while his friends row past the Sirens with wax in their ears. The hero apparently enjoys the music, but the Sirens' spell is broken and they commit suicide by diving headlong into the sea.*

LEFT *J M W Turner (1775–1851),* Ulysses Deriding Polyphemus. *Polyphemus can just be seen in the misty light above the ship of Odysseus (Ulysses). Ghostly Nereids swim ahead of the ship, which is portrayed as a fantastic galleon. From the rigging flies a flag (hardly visible) depicting the Trojan horse outside the Trojan walls, referring to Odysseus' victory. Every feature of the painting veers between fantasy and reality: the arched rocks at times appear to be horses' heads rearing from the sea to pull the sun-chariot into the sky. A masterly Romantic treatment of the Classical myth.*

cial herb which would act as an antidote to Circe's drugs. Odysseus slipped it into the wine which Circe offered him; he then drew his sword and threatened to kill her unless she turned his friends back into human form. She obliged and after much feasting welcomed Odysseus into her bed. The Greek heroes stayed with Circe for a year; when they left, Circe advised Odysseus to visit the prophet Teiresias in Hades, for only a wise man could tell the Greeks how they might appease the gods and return home safely.

Circe had also warned Odysseus about other monsters who inhabited that part of the Mediterranean. These included the Sirens, women with the feet and wings of birds, who sang songs of such seductive beauty that many sailors had been lured to their rocky island, where they wasted away in yearning for the music. Odysseus wanted to hear the song and instructed the crew to row past the island with wax in their ears; he himself was lashed to the mast. The Sirens, fated to die if they were ever unsuccessful, crashed to their deaths in the sea below.

LEFT *Dosso Dossi (1474/9–1542),* Circe and her Lovers in a Landscape, *(c1525). Circe's woodland palace can be seen in the background. She holds a stone tablet inscribed with spells; a book lies at her feet with a magic pentagram on the open page. Dossi has transformed the Classical sorceress into a beautiful medieval witch.*

After many more adventures, Odysseus at last arrived at his home in Ithaca where his wife Penelope had been waiting for many years. While her husband was away she had been approached by princes from all over the Mediterranean who were intent upon marrying her. She refused to believe their false stories that Odysseus was dead, and told them that she would consider their offers only when she had finished weaving a funerary shroud for her father-in-law; every night she would unravel the day's work to delay its completion. Odysseus, disguised as a beggar, had arranged a contest for the suitors: they must string the bow of the absent Odysseus and fire an arrow through a row of twelve axe-heads; the prize would be Penelope. None of them were even able to string the bow and they all jeered at the beggar when he asked to have a go. Odysseus strung the bow with ease and his first arrow flew through each of the axe-heads; with the remaining arrows he killed the suitors.

ABOVE Penelope and Odysseus; black-figure skyphos (wine-cup), late 6th century BC. A burlesque version of the myth: Penelope is shown beside her loom with the unfinished shroud; she mixes a drink for her returned husband in a cup of the same shape as the vase itself.

Oedipus and the Sphinx

Oedipus' name means 'swollen foot': his father, King Laius of Thebes, had been told by an oracle that his son would one day kill him; therefore when his wife Jocasta gave birth to a boy, he was taken (as was the custom for unwanted children) into the mountains and exposed after having his feet pierced. A shepherd found the boy and took him to Corinth, where the childless king and queen adopted the boy, whom they called Oedipus because of his injured feet. One evening, when he had become a man, a drunken friend told

Oedipus that the king and queen were not his true parents. Oedipus could not rest until he had travelled to Delphi and asked the Pythia how he could find his real mother and father; the oracle replied that it would be better if he had not made the enquiry, for one day he would murder his father and make love to his mother. Oedipus in dismay decided never to return to Corinth in order to avoid the prophecy, for he still believed that the kind king and queen were his true parents; instead he made his way to Thebes. At a three-way junction in the road called the Cleft Way, a chariot approached Oedipus and the driver rudely shouted to Oedipus to get off the road. Oedipus' royal honour was wounded and he killed both charioteer and passenger.

When Oedipus arrived at Thebes he heard that a female monster, the Sphinx, had become a menace to the city. News of the death of King Laius on the roadside at the Cleft Way was brought to Creon, who was acting as regent in the absence of the king. Creon promised the hand of the king's widow, Jocasta, in marriage to any man who killed the Sphinx. Oedipus, with nothing to lose, decided to make the attempt. The Sphinx would fly onto the ramparts of the city and set a riddle to anyone she found there; if they were unable to answer it, she would eat them. Oedipus waited by the ramparts for the arrival of the monster, who asked him: 'What creature walks on four legs in the morning, on two at noon, and on three in the evening?' Clever Oedipus answered:

LEFT Oedipus and the Sphinx; Athenian red-figure wine-cup by the Oedipus Painter, early 5th century BC. Oedipus is shown in travelling clothes and sun-hat; he is depicted with the 'thoughtful' gestures of crossed legs and hand to chin. The scene would have appeared as the drinker drained his cup.

RIGHT Girodet-Trioson (1767–1824), The Sleep of Endymion. The painter studied with David, whose cool severity can be seen here. However, there is an aspect of dreamy Romanticism already at work and Girodet-Trioson was admired by many early Romantics. Selene is present only as the light of the moon which Eros ushers into the woodland cave of the beautiful sleeping king.

'The creature is man, for he crawls on all fours as a baby, walks on his two legs for most of his adult life, and resorts to a walking-stick in his retirement.' The Sphinx jumped to her death and Oedipus was welcomed as the new Theban hero and married Jocasta.

A new plague came to Thebes and Oedipus sent Creon to the Pythia to ask advice; she answered that the plague would not cease until Laius' murderer was exiled from the city. The prophet Teiresias was consulted, and unhappy Oedipus learnt the truth: he had killed his father on the Cleft Way and married his mother; the shepherd, who years ago had saved him from exposure, was called in as a witness to the truth of the prophet's words. Jocasta hanged herself and Oedipus, realizing his blindness to the truth, gouged out his own eyes. After his death he was buried outside of Athens by Theseus, who had learnt that the hero's tomb would protect the city.

TALES OF TRAGIC ROMANCE

Selene and Endymion

Endymion was a grandson of Zeus and founded the city of Elis, where he became king. Selene, who took the moon across the sky in her chariot, saw Endymion by the light of the moon one night and fell in love with him, for he was very handsome. Every night the two would meet in a cave and make love in the moonlight. Selene was so in love with Endymion that she could not bear to see his mortal beauty wane with age. Therefore one night, instead of visiting him in the cave, she touched his eyes with magic moondrops and put him to sleep for eternity. Every night she continues to gaze upon her lover from her chariot in the sky.

Cephalus and Procris

Cephalus, the Prince of Phocis, came to Athens to marry Procris, the daughter of King Erectheus. Cephalus would go out hunting very early and one morning was abducted by Eos the Dawn; he protested that he could not love the goddess, for he was betrothed to his mortal lover Procris. Eos threw him back down to earth, saying that he would regret his refusal of divine love. Cephalus suffered from a terrible jealousy of his lovely wife and would test her fidelity by trying to seduce her in the guise of a stranger. One day, however, Procris was told that her husband had been heard shouting the name of a woman named Aura while out hunting in the woods. Procris followed her husband next time he went hunting and hid in the bushes. Cephalus hurled his infallible javelin at what he thought was the rustling of a wild boar; as she lay dying in his arms he realized her grave mistake: he had indeed been calling on Aura, which means 'breeze', to cool his heated brow.

Achilles and Penthesileia

The mortal Peleus married the immortal Nereid Thetis. They were unaware that this marriage had been arranged by the gods who had been told that if Thetis were to have a son by a divine father, he would one day rule Olympus. All important gods and men were invited to the wedding feast; but Eris (Strife) was not invited, and she thought up an act of revenge which was to have dire and long-lasting consequences for mankind. She inscribed a golden apple with the words 'FOR THE MOST BEAUTIFUL' and cast it at the feet of the goddesses Hera, Athene and Aphrodite as they were coming home. They all claimed it, but Zeus suggested a beauty contest judged by the most beautiful man on earth, Paris, Prince of Troy. Each goddess tried to bribe the judge, and Aphrodite succeeded by offering him the most beautiful woman on earth as

LEFT *Claude Lorraine
(1600–82),*
Landscape with
Cephalus and Procris
Reunited by Diana.
*Claude has typically
chosen a Classical
subject which requires a
landscape. There is
little sense of the
impending doom of the
myth in the idyllic and
peaceful pastoral
setting. The buildings
are taken from the
countryside around
Rome which Claude
loved.*

RIGHT Achilles kills
Penthesilea; *Athenian
black-figure amphora
potted and painted by
Exekias, mid 6th
century BC. Exekias
epoiese ('Exekias
made this') is signed to
the left of Achilles.
Exekias has brilliantly
evoked the tragedy by
making the line of the
spear run parallel to the
eyes as the lovers meet
for the first and last
time.*

FAR RIGHT Achilles and
Penthesilea; *Athenian
black-figure vase, 6th
century BC. Achilles
carries the dead
Amazon off the
battlefield, her limbs
limp and her eyes
closed in death.*

his wife: this was Helen, the wife of Menelaus of Sparta. Paris visited Sparta and abducted Helen, taking her back to Troy. Menelaus and his brother Agamemnon, together with other Greek kings, besieged Troy for nine years.

Penthesileia was an Amazon queen who had accidentally killed one of her sisters. King Priam of Troy offered her purification if she would bring Amazon troops to help him fight the Greeks. One day she was out fighting on the Trojan plain when Achilles, son of Peleus and Thetis and King of the Myrmidons, singled her out in combat. They struggled for hours until at last Achilles drove his spear into her throat; at that moment his eyes met hers and he fell deeply in love with her, carrying her lifeless body from the battlefield in his grief.

The Greeks won the war and sacked Troy, but many of them died for Helen, including Achilles, who was shot by an arrow in the ankle, his one vulnerable point. One ancient tradition says that Thetis had dipped him as a child in the river Styx to make him immortal, but had forgotten to immerse the ankle by which she was holding him.

BELOW *Peter Paul Rubens (1577–1640), The Judgement of Paris. Paris, accompanied by Hermes, awards the golden apple to Aphrodite. To her right is Hera with her sacred peacock and to the left is Athene, armour laid aside; the Medusa head is here placed on her shield and not the aegis. In the sky appears the Fury, Alecto, symbolizing the tragedy to come.*

Aphrodite and Adonis

The beautiful youth Adonis was born from the incestuous union of Myrrha with her own father Cinyras, King of Assyria. Aphrodite had caused this because the Assyrian queen had boasted that Myrrha was prettier than the goddess of love. Aphrodite fell in love with the young Adonis and handed him to Persephone to look after; but Persephone also desired Adonis and refused to return her charge. Zeus chose the Muse Calliope as an arbitrator and she judged that the two rival goddesses must share their lover. Some say that Aphrodite wreaked her revenge on Calliope for her decision by engineering the death of her son Orpheus. In any case, the story ends with the tragic, early death of Adonis during a wild boar hunt – perhaps the victim of Hephaestus or Ares, jealous husband and lover of Aphrodite. To commemorate her lover, the goddess created the red anemone flower from his blood.

Hylas and the Nymphs

On his voyage with the Argonauts to find the Golden Fleece, Heracles took with him a handsome boy as a travelling companion: his name was Hylas and he became Heracles' lover. During the journey, the heroes beached the magical ship *Argo* at Mysia in order to cut some new oars from the trees by the shore; Heracles sent Hylas off in search of fresh water. Hylas made his way slowly through the wild undergrowth, listening for the sound of running water. It was not long before he found himself lost, but he had discovered a clear pool and he leant over the still water to fill his jug. To his astonishment he found himself gazing into the eyes of several lovely Naiads, the nymphs who inhabited the lonely spring. In an instant, he felt himself being drawn down into the water to become the nymphs eternal lover. Heracles was heartbroken and roamed the woods for days crying for his lost friend.

Pyramus and Thisbe

In the city of Babylon there lived next door to one another two rival families. Pyramus had been a friend of his neighbour, Thisbe, since childhood, but as they grew older their respective parents forbade them to meet. Their bedrooms were next to each other and Pyramus managed to knock a small hole in the wall through which they could kiss and whisper. They fell in love and decided to marry against their parents' wishes. So, one night they arranged to meet by a tomb outside the city walls. Thisbe arrived first wearing a wedding veil; while she was waiting a lioness came to drink at a nearby pool – it was thirsty after a meal and its jaws were dripping with blood. Thisbe was alarmed and ran into a cave for shelter, dropping her veil in her haste. The lioness sprang after her but found only the veil which became stained by the bloody mane of the beast.

At last Pyramus arrived at their meeting place, only to discover the blood-stained veil and the paw-prints of the lioness. In his grief, Pyramus stabbed himself with his sword, staining the white fruit of the mulberry tree, which stood at the trysting-place, red. Thisbe, leaving her hiding place, found her lover dead and killed herself with Pyramus' sword.

Their parents were so stricken by the tragic deaths that they swore friendship and buried their children's ashes in a single urn. Two local rivers were named after the lovers and the mulberry tree continues to bear blood-red fruit to this day.

STORIES OF METAMORPHOSIS

Narcissus

Narcissus was the son of the nymph Leiriope and the river Cephissus. Leriope consulted Teiresias, the pro-

RIGHT Pyramus and Thisbe; *Roman wall-painting from a Pompeian House, 1st century* AD. *Thisbe kills herself on discovering her dead lover. The painting decorated an outdoor dining-couch and was coupled with a painting of Narcissus. Both stories were described in the 'Metamorphoses' of the contemporary poet Ovid, and it is likely that the paintings reflect the poem's popularity.*

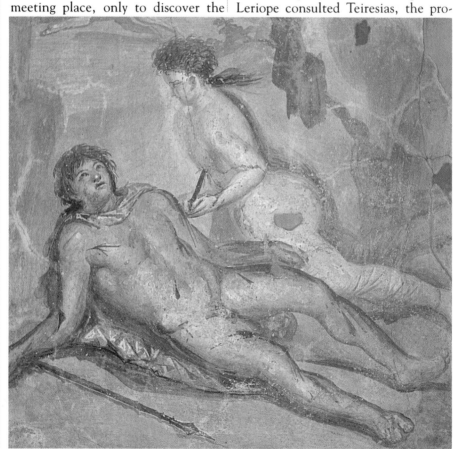

phet, and asked him if Narcissus would have a long life; Teiresias replied that he would so long as he did not know himself. Narcissus was admired by many girls and boys, but never returned their love. One, a nymph called Echo, fell hopelessly in love with Narcissus when she spied him hunting in the woods where she lived. Echo also suffered another affliction: her task had been to divert Hera's attentin with her constant chatter while her friends pursued their love affairs with Zeus, and, when found out, Hera punished her for her talkativeness by taking away her ability to utter anything but the last words of other people's sentences. Thus, unable to express her feelings for Narcissus, she

had wasted away with unrequited love until she was merely a voice.

One boy prayed to Nemesis, the goddess of retribution, to punish Narcissus for his arrogance. One day, Narcissus was hunting on the slopes of Mount Helicon when he came to a clear pool; he stooped to quench his thirst and immediately fell in love with the beautiful boy reflected in the calm water. However much he talked to or tried to embrace him, the boy would not respond, but Narcissus would not leave his love and faded away like Echo, dying of starvation. The gold-centred, white-petalled flower that we call narcissus was all that remained when his friends discovered him by the pool.

BELOW John Waterhouse (1849–1917), Echo and Narcissus, (c1903). A rather thin and wasted Echo gazes longingly at Narcissus who has laid aside his quiver to admire his own reflection in the pool, located in a very English-looking water meadow. By the boy's feet appear the flowers to which he will give his name.

Baucis and Philemon

Baucis and Philemon were a poor, elderly peasant couple who lived in a hillside cottage in Bithynia. As Zeus and Hermes were wandering through this land, everywhere they went refused them hospitality. As the sun was setting they came to the old couple's home and were cordially welcomed. During the simple meal, Baucis and Philemon realized that their guests were not ordinary men since their wine-cups kept miraculously refilling. The next day the gods showed them the hostile village below: it was now a lake and their cottage was transformed into a beautiful marble temple. Granted a wish, Baucis and Philemon asked only to serve the gods in their new temple. When they died the loving couple were turned into an old oak and a linden tree to commemorate their goodness.

BELOW Rembrandt van Rijn (1606–1669), Philemon and Baucis, (1658). Rembrandt treats the myth with great compassion, sensitively depicting the humble behaviour of the poor old couple in the presence of gods, who appear genuinely moved by their piety. The artist's skill at using the 'chiaroscuro' (light and shade) technique to create a wondrous atmosphere is most evident here.

Apollo and Daphne

Daphne was a young Arcadian girl who used to hunt with her friends along the banks of the river Ladon. She worshipped the virgin goddess of hunting, Artemis, and had chosen to remain chaste herself. Eros assisted her chastity by firing a lead-tipped arrow into her heart; at the same time he shot Apollo with a gold-tipped arrow because the god had taunted him by telling him to leave archery to real men. Apollo fell in love with Daphne and pursued her through the woods; Daphne, realizing that she could not escape the god, prayed to Gaia for help. Gaia responded and transformed her into a laurel (Daphne means laurel). All that Apollo was left with was a branch torn from the lovely tree, which he placed as a wreath in his hair. The laurel tree remained sacred to Apollo.

RIGHT Giovanni Battista Tiepolo (1696–1770), Apollo Pursuing Daphne, (c1775–1760). Tiepolo depicts Daphne stumbling into a river-god with Eros hiding from the angry Apollo. The sun is behind Apollo's head and he already wears the laurel which begins to sprout from Daphne's hands.

Zeus and Io

Io was a priestess of Hera at Argos. Zeus was attracted by her beauty and probably by the possibilities of annoying his wife Hera. He came and whispered to her in her dreams, inviting her to the meadows where her father, the local river-god Inachus, watched over his cattle. Io told her father of her strange dreams, and he sent enquiries to various oracles, all of which replied that Io must go into exile or the city would be destroyed by a huge thunderbolt. Io departed in low spirits but as she was passing through the river meadows Zeus approached; but Hera saw him from her temple and Zeus in his embarrassment turned Io into a beautiful white cow. Hera saw through the ruse and demanded the cow for herself, which she had tethered in an olive-grove at Mycenae and watched over by Argus Panoptes (All-Seeing), who had 100 eyes.

In retaliation, Zeus sent Hermes as god of thieves to steal the cow; Hermes, in the guise of a goatherd, played a lullaby on his pipes and soon all of Argus's eyes were closed. Hermes

RIGHT *Pieter Lastman (1583–1633), Juno discovering Jupiter with Io, (1618). Hera (Juno) appears with her peacocks (with the eyes of the dead Argus in their tails), outraged at her husband Zeus' (Jupiter) attempts to carry off Io, who he has transformed into a cow. The masked figure with the fox-pelt is a symbol of sly deceit.*

killed the guard, but Hera took Argus's eyes and placed them in the tail of her sacred bird, the peacock; she then sent a gadfly to sting the cow which broke away and escaped. After many months of wandering the cow arrived in Egypt and, beside the river Nile, Zeus made love to her in the guise of a bull. Io found herself a woman again and gave birth to a boy whom she named Epaphus ('touch of the god'); but jealous Hera sent the demon youths, the Curetes, to kidnap her son and take him to Syria. Zeus in his fury killed the Curetes even though they had once helped to protect him from his angry father when he was a boy in Crete. Io was guided to Epaphus and returned with him to Egypt where she married King Telegonus and instituted the worship of Demeter. Later Egyptians worshipped both Demeter and Io as Isis.

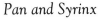

Pan and Syrinx

Syrinx was a woodland nymph who hunted in the forests of Arcadia with the goddess Artemis. The lecherous Pan, son of Hermes, who also lived in Arcadia, saw Syrinx one day as she ran past his cave pursuing a stag. He chased after her and Syrinx, who had vowed to the virgin Artemis that she would remain chaste, cried out to the nymphs of the River Ladon to help her. They quickly transformed her into a reed-bed, and when Pan reached the river all he found were the reeds swaying in the breeze. He cut them down, and trimmed them to different lengths to produce varied notes and bound them together in a row to make a set of pipes. He called these pipes 'syrinx' to commemorate his unfulfilled love.

STORIES OF DIVINE RETRIBUTION

Dionysus and Pentheus

The story forms the basis of The Bacchae, *a tragedy written by the playwright Euripides, when Classical Athens was at the height of its imperial power. It celebrates the introduction of a foreign religion into a highly conservative culture. The Dionysiac religion demanded irrationality in its devotees. This was highly disturbing to the normal rational thinking of Greek intellectuals, but worship of the god of wine was eventually welcomed as an essential part of human experience. A major annual festival was devoted to him at Athens, during which large terracotta phalli were carried in magnificent processions to his temple by* the Acropolis. *Nearby was the open-air theatre, in which tragedies (such as* The Bacchae) *were performed in his honour. Dionysus was also worshipped in the more intimate circumstances of the 'symposium', or drinking party, during which members of the Athenian elite would be joined by 'hetairai', courtesans who would sing poetry and entertain with sexual favours. During these orgiastic rites, the males would identify with the Satyrs, woodland followers of the god who were part goat or horse; the females would become Maenads or Bacchae; they wore fawn or panther skins and carried 'thyrsoi', wands wound with ivy and tipped with pine cones. Ivy or oak leaves were worn in their hair, and they danced wild, ecstatic dances in adoration of the god.*

Near the walled city of Thebes, on Mount Cithaeron, frenzied royal ladies roamed aimlessly. They included the sisters of Semele, mother of Dionysus, the beautiful youth who had not been

BELOW *Velazquez (1599–1660),* The Topers, *(c1629). Velazquez has typically mixed the Classical idealized figures of Dionysus and follower with realistically portrayed contemporary Spanish peasants.*

seen since his strange and miraculous birth. One of his aunts, Agave, was the mother of Pentheus the King of Thebes. The people of Thebes had refused to acknowledge the godhead in Dionysus, who had returned to his home after gathering devotees and establishing his cult throughout Asia. His devotees were the Maenads or Bacchae, Asian women who celebrated the god wherever he drove them, tempting the local women to abandon their husbands and homes and join them outside the city walls in orgiastic celebrations of wild nature. The rational Greek mind did not understand them and Pentheus suspected political rebellion. The Theban women had been driven mad by Dionysus for refusing to believe in him; on the mountain slopes they joined in with the song of the Bacchae:

From the high hills of Asia, exotic
    Mount Tmolus
We run and we run and we cannot stop
    running
Rejoicing in hard work and loving our
    leisure
Driven by Bacchus, his beauty and
    laughter.

Anyone present who's not of the god
Stay away from our ritual and keep
    your doors bolted
No listening, no peeping, O why don't
    you join us?
It's heavenly dancing the dance of the
    god.

Happy the man who seeks the wild
    country
Turning his back on the city of dreams;
His head crowned with ivy, not jewel-
    studded gold,
A branch for a sceptre, a heart for a
    stone.

His ecstacy drives us from out of the
    hills
Down into the city, the streets paved
    with stone,
Bringing the joys of the god born of
    god
Dancing the dreams of the spirit of
    wine.

Meanwhile, in the city of Thebes, Pentheus had heard news of these strange happenings; members of his family had already joined the cult, and both his mother Agave and his grandfather Cadmus attempted to persuade Pentheus to join them and welcome the new god Dionysus into their city. The seer Teiresias also joined the cult.

Pentheus, fearing that this irrational worship might lead to anarchy in his city, had the young priest (Dionysus in disguise) arrested and interrogated him. He mocked his feminine softness and beautiful hair and threw him into prison. Dionysus miraculously broke the lock and appeared to Pentheus, who thus reaized his power. Dionysus tempted the young king to come and watch the Maenads performing their orgiastic dances; but he would have to go in secret, dressed as one of the women.

Dionysus then led Pentheus to the mountain, where he spied on the Maenads. One of them caught sight of the interloper and, together with her friends, chased him through the woods, thinking him a wild animal. They caught him and tore him to bits; Agave came back to Thebes with her victim's head as a trophy of her victory in the hunt. She showed the prize to Cadmus, who immediately realized her error.

LEFT The death of Pentheus; *Roman wall-painting from the House of the Vettii, Pompeii, 1st century* AD. *This is possibly a copy of an earlier Greek original.*

Artemis and Actaeon

The story of Actaeon and his macabre fate remained a favourite with poets and artists throughout the Classical period. The nature of his punishment by Artemis remains the same, but his crime differs. Early writers say that he offended Zeus by wanting to marry the mortal Semele, who was pregnant with Zeus' child Dionysus, the god of wine. In the Classical period we see him boasting that he is a better hunter than Artemis. Hellenistic poets present him as a lusty and unashamed voyeur of the bathing goddess, deserving his punishment. The Roman poet Ovid, however, protests his innocence; he stumbled unawares upon the divinity and her retribution was therefore doubly cruel. The myth was particularly popular with wall-painters in Imperial Pompeii.

Actaeon hunted the stag. One morning he was woken by the full moon gazing in through the palace windows and the baying of his favourite pair of hounds. He swallowed cool water, threw on his cloak and, armed with spears, unlatched the kennel doors. Out they ran, Tracker and Blackfoot, their puppies Lightfoot and Tigress – their first hunt – and the old ones Storm and Blanche.

Outside the palace walls, the hounds veered from their usual direction. Turning tails on the rosy-fingered goddess of dawn, Eos, they headed for the pearly light of Artemis, goddess of the moon and the chase. Cool cypresses shadowed the path which soon led to tractless woodland and wilderness. Wild bramble gave place to apple. Actaeon stretched to taste the fruit, expecting bitterness; strange sweetness. Then great thirst and a search for water.

RIGHT *Titian (1478/90–1576)*, The Death of Actaeon. *Beneath a stormy sky, Artemis (Diana) is shown loosing an arrow at stag-headed Actaeon, whose hounds have brought him down beside a woodland stream. Artemis is depicted with one breast bare in the manner of the Amazons.*

The hounds arrived first and were soon curled up asleep beside the stream. Actaeon had a desire to bathe and made his way towards the sound of falling water. Storm, wise and grizzled, raised and lowered an eyelid and returned to dreaming of stags. Actaeon approached the pool alone, but sounds of unearthly laughter stopped him in his tracks. Breath held – distant thunder – a splash – cautious peeping through the tangled branches. Actaeon's heart raced, he had spied the Dryads before, but always from the corner of his eye and never in the presence of the horned goddess. In an instant Actaeon was infatuated by Artemis the huntress, never before seen unclothed by mortal or indeed immortal eyes. The nymphs were merely stars in the presence of her glistening lunar beauty.

Artemis sensed the alien and threw water at his gaze. As his sight slowly returned, Actaeon felt panic. The pool, now still, mirrored his transformation. Even as he watched his forehead sprouted antlers, his feet and hands became furry hooves, and his neck extended. Blackfoot and Tracker woke to their master's musky scent and led the pack downstream. Actaeon, knowing his fate, attempted a scream and took to his heels. His hounds heard only the deep roar of the hunted stag and· were hungry for the kill. Actaeon the hunter now knew, as he scrambled on all fours, what it felt like to be the hunted one.

He ran swiftly and came at last to a clearing in the forest. He stood, head held high, sniffing the damp night air. His hounds, as he himself had trained them, came at him from all sides, giving no quarter. Blackfoot and Tracker were the first. Actaeon tried to pat them as they jumped, but their enthusiasm was not the joy of greeting a master. They sank their teeth in deep, howling to their companions to join the feast. In the evening, beneath a crimson hunter's moon, the hounds sought in vain for their master. The horse-man Cheiron heard their sad howling and fashioned a statue of Actaeon to comfort them. This was set in the woodland shrine of Artemis, goddess of wildlife, as a reminder of her power.

Hermes alone among men and gods can pass unharmed between Heaven and Earth, or Earth and Hades. That same evening he escorted sad Actaeon through the gates which divide the living from the dead. Cerberus, triple-headed watchdog of the Underworld, had been trained by his master, Hades, to terrify only the proud. On this occasion he sensed the fear of dogs and Actaeon had safe passage.

Daedalus and Icarus

Daedalus was a great craftsman and inventor who had been exiled from his home in Athens to Crete where King Minos employed him as his architect. When Theseus killed the Minotaur, Minos had Daedalus and his son Icarus imprisoned in the Labyrinth for their part in the plot. They escaped by making pairs of wings held together with bees-wax and were flying westwards when Icarus, who had been warned by his father to stay in the middle of the sky, flew upwards towards Helius. The sun-god, angry at the boy's attempts to approach the realms of the gods, melted the wax and Icarus crashed down into the sea which still bears his name, the Icarian Sea. His body was washed ashore on Icaria, where Heracles later buried him.

ABOVE *Pieter Brueghel the Elder (c1525–69), The Fall of Icarus. The ploughman and shepherd continue their everyday work as Icarus falls into the sea in the lower right-hand corner of this expansive Northern European landscape; even the fisherman appears not to notice the crash beside him. The sun, which caused Icarus's death, is only just rising on the horizon.*

Laocoon

Laocoon, the Trojan priest of Poseidon, warned the Trojans not to accept gifts from the Greeks. One morning, they awoke to discover a huge wooden horse, which they thought must be a divine offering. Laocoon was suspicious and hurled his spear into the side of the horse; at that moment, two sea-serpents, at the command of Apollo whom Laocoon had once insulted, rose out of the sea and strangled the priest along with his two sons. Laocoon's fears were confirmed when the horse was dragged into the city: it contained Greek troops who emerged in the night and began the terrible sack of Troy.

Apollo and Marsyas

When Perseus killed the Gorgon Medusa, Athene was amazed at the strange sounds of lamentation made by her remaining sisters. She made a musical instrument which imitated their mournful notes: this was the 'aulos', a double flute played by blowing hard through a thin reed.

One day, as she played the aulos, Athene saw her face reflected in a pool and dismayed at the image of her contorted face, threw the pipes to the ground. Marsyas, a satyr, had been listening to her play from the bushes and tip-toed forward to claim the rejected aulos. He learnt to play it and challenged Apollo to a musical contest; the victor would win the right to use the other in whatever way he chose. The Muses were appointed as judges, but could not decide on a winner. Apollo then played his lyre upside down and challenged Marsyas to do the same. This was an impossible feat on the aulos and Apollo was declared the victor by default. Apollo claimed the prize, and he punished the satyr's audacity by tying him to a pine tree and flaying him alive.

BELOW *Domenichino (1582–1641), The Flaying of Marsyas. The artist, who worked in Rome, portrays the scene in a Roman countryside, with a medieval hill town in the background, and Italian shepherds mournfully observing the punishment.*

RIGHT *El Greco (1541–1614), Laocoon (c1610). The violent subject, with its contorted, writhing figures provides a fitting subject for El Greco's anti-naturalistic style. However, though the figures are unnaturalistic, a real horse, representing the artificial wooden horse, approaches a medieval-looking Troy. On the left stand several figures, looking on helplessly like a Greek Tragic Chorus.*

FIVE

The Constellations

Ancient Greek cartographers combined their researches in mapping the earth with the drawing of star charts. Unable to make any rational sense of the night sky, they equated the movements of the planets with various gods and imagined that the stars had been set into patterns by the gods to immortalize mythical characters. The early Greek astronomers, limited to the naked eye, saw only five planets which they associated with different gods according to their behaviour: Hermes (Mercury) moved swiftly; Ares (Mars) was blood-red and associated with war; Aphrodite (Venus) was bright and flirtatious; Zeus (Jupiter) moved majestically across the heavens; Cronus (Saturn) was dim, slow moving and distant – a nostalgic sign of the Golden Age.

The Milky Way, like many of the constellations (literally, 'star groups') was interpreted in several ways: the fiery gash burnt across the heavens by Phaethon when he drove his father Helius' chariot out of control or the stairway to heaven. The ancient astronomers also noted that the sun passed through twelve of their constellations, which became the signs of the Zodiac.

Andromeda, Cepheus and Cassiopeia

Cepheus and Cassiopeia, King and Queen of the Ethiopians, boasted that their daughter, Andromeda, was more beautiful than the Nereids, daughters of Nereus, the Old Man of the Sea. This act of hybris incurred the wrath of Poseidon who sent out one of his many sea-monsters to devastate the coastlands of Ethiopia. King Cepheus was advised by an oracle that there was only one way that he might placate the god's anger; he must sacrifice his daughter to the monster. Andromeda was bound with chains at the foot of a cliff, waiting for the tide to come in bringing the sea-monster; but the hero Perseus rescued her and took her home to Argolis in Greece where she bore him many children. Cepheus and Cassiopeia mourned the loss of their daughter and Poseidon, considering that they had been sufficiently punished, took pity on them by placing them in the heavens. Andromeda missed her parents and therefore, when she died,

Athene also placed her among the stars, beside them. However, as an eternal warning against human pride, Poseidon has placed Cassiopeia on a chair, but upside down with her feet in the air.

Aquarius the Water-Bearer and Aquila the Eagle

People argue as to the mortal parentage of the young Trojan prince Ganymede, but whoever his father, he had the misfortune of being so beautiful as to attract the gods themselves. One day Zeus decided to have him brought to Olympus to be his own personal cup-bearer; hitherto Hebe had performed this task for all the gods. Zeus could never appear on earth as himself for his lightning-bolts would incinerate any mortal, but neither could he trust his fellow gods to abduct Ganymede on his behalf. So Zeus disguised himself as an eagle and flew down to Troy, where he swooped down on Ganymede and, grasping the boy in his talons, took him back across the sea to Olympus.

BELOW *Piero di Cosimo (1462–1521), Perseus Rescuing Andromeda (c1510). Piero has incorporated several episodes into the one painting: on the left the onlookers turn their heads aside in fear as the sea-monster approaches Andromeda. Perseus is shown both flying in from the right and standing on the monster's back swinging his sword. On the right, the king and queen receive their daughter and her new heroic husband to the sounds of music and rejoicing.*

ABOVE Zeus and
Ganymede; *terracotta
temple roof sculpture
from Olympia, early
5th century* BC. *Traces
of the paint which
covered many clay and
marble statues in the
Classical world can be
clearly seen on this
lively group. Though
bearing many Archaic
features, the group has
been dated to the Early
Classical period.*

To console the parents for the loss, Zeus ordered the divine messenger Hermes to deliver to them a splendid gift: this was a grapevine of gold, the handiwork of Hephaestus. They continued to miss their fine son, so Zeus immortalized Ganymede's abduction by placing Ganymede and the eagle (Aquila) up amongst the stars for all to see at night.

Aries the Ram

Athamas was King of the Orchomenus in Boeotia. In spite of his great wealth he was one of the most unlucky men who ever lived. His children by his first wife Nephele were Phrixus and Helle; he took a second wife Ino, who also bore sons and she plotted to destroy Phrixus so that one of her own sons might succeed Athamas as king. Ino talked the Boeotian women who sow the grain seeds into parching it so that the next harvest was a disaster; Athamas sent messengers to seek advice from the oracle at Delphi; on the way back they were bribed by Ino into delivering a false report that Phrixus must be sacrificed in order to avert famine.

Athamas reluctantly led his son to the altar of Zeus and raised the ritual knife to cut his throat; just at that moment a ram appeared and, with Phrixus and his sister Helle on its back, flew off towards the east.

On the journey they discovered that the creature could talk, and the beautiful ram whose fleece was of gleaming gold told them stories: he had been born to Poseidon and Theophane; Theophane had been turned into a ewe by Poseidon in order to fool her many suitors, so naturally Poseidon made love to her in the guise of a ram. As they flew over the straits where the Black Sea is joined to the Mediterranean, Helle lost her grip and fell into the sea; the straits are called the Hellespont in her honour. Eventually Phrixus landed at Colchis at the other end of the Black Sea, where the ram insisted that he sacrifice it and hang its golden fleece on an oak in a grove sacred to Ares the war god. Phrixus married a local princess and lived to a ripe old age, and he never forgot the ram who had saved his life; it was immortalized as the constellation Aries and the reason that its stars shine so dimly is that its shining fleece remained on earth, the object of the heroic quest of Jason and the Argonauts.

Auriga (The Charioteer)

The bright star Capella appears to stand behind two pairs of lesser stars. The Greeks realized that this represented the immortalized souls of a charioteer and his four horses, but could never agree on who it was: some said Erichthonius, legendary king of Athens; others Myrtilus, son of Hermes, who was bribed by Pelops to replace the lynch-pins of his master Oenomaus's chariot with wax so as to cause his death.

Cancer (The Crab)

Cancer lived in a swamp with the monstrous Hydra and when Heracles came along to kill her as one of his labours, the crab tried to help his friend by biting the hero's foot. Though this was unsuccessful, Hera rewarded the crab by transforming it into the constellation Cancer.

Capricorn

Aegipan (Goat-Pan) was the son of Zeus and a goat called Aex, whose skin Zeus took for his aegis when she died. In his battle with the monster Typhon, Zeus had lost his sinews which Typhon then hid. Aegipan and Hermes recovered their father's sinews, but Typhon chased them into Egypt where they disguised themselves by changing shapes; Aegipan turned his lower half into a fish to make his escape by sea. Zeus showed his gratitude by placing him in the heavens as the constellation Capricorn; he still has the top half of a goat and a fish's tail.

RIGHT The Punishment of Ixion; Roman wall-painting from The House of the Vettii, Pompeii, 1st century AD. Probably a copy of a lost Late Classical Greek easel-painting. Hera (right) observes the punishment; Iris (or Hebe) stands behind and wears a 'nimbus', the divine aura which became the halo of Christian art; Nephele, the cloud-copy of Hera, sits below. Hermes, in the pose of a Classical sculpture, is about to wheel Ixion down to Hades (the dark bearded figure).

The Centaur

The first centaur was Centaurus who was born from the union of the mortal Ixion and Nephele, a cloud that Zeus had substituted for his wife Hera when Ixion had dared to make love to her. Ixion was taken to Hades; he was lashed to a fiery wheel and rolled forever around the Underworld.

Centaurus, with his human head, arms and shoulders and body of a horse, represented the lustful side of man's nature, and the centaurs were often used in art to symbolize non-Greek, uncivilized barbarians. The centaur Cheiron was different; he was the son of Cronus and the Oceanid Philyra; in order to deceive his wife Rhea, Cronus turned into a stallion to make love to Philyra, but Rhea discovered them and Philyra fled to mountainous Pelasgia where she bore her strange child, who had a stallion's body from waist downwards. Zeus turned Philyra into a linden tree, but she need not have been ashamed of her son, for Cheiron, unlike Centaurus' descendants, became so wise and learned that many young Greeks were sent to be educated by him on Mount Pelion where he lived; these included Actaeon, Achilles and Jason. Cheiron was immortalized as the constellation named Centaur.

Canis Major and Canis Minor (The Great Dog and The Little Dog)

The larger of the two dogs was the hound of Orion the Hunter; the bright star Sirius (the dog star) was seen as a sign of coming droughts when it rose along with the smaller dog. The little dog was Maera, faithful hound of Icarius, the Athenian who was sent by Dionysus to introduce the gift of wine to the world; but the shepherds who received the first cups took it unwatered and clubbed Icarius to death for attempting to poison them, throwing his body into a well. Maera ran to fetch Icarius' daughter Erigone, who hanged herself from a tree above the well; poor Maera leapt into the well to join his master.

Cetus (The Whale)

This sea-monster was sent by Poseidon to devour Andromeda as a punishment for the boastings of her mother Cassiopeia; it was killed by the hero Perseus and appears alongside him and Andromeda.

ABOVE *Titian (1478/
90–1576), Bacchus
and Ariadne.
Dionysus (Bacchus)
leaps down from his
leopard-drawn chariot.
The god is followed by
his Maenads and
Satyrs who play music
and hold the torn limbs
of their animal prey.
Ariadne's crown
appears above her as
the constellation
Corona Borealis.*

Corona Borealis
(The Northern Crown)

Ariadne received a glittering crown as a divine wedding gift, either from her earthly husband Theseus, presented by the Nereid Thetis, or from her divine lover Dionysus, presented by Aphrodite; it was Dionysus who set its jewels in the night sky to immortalize his love for Ariadne.

Corvus (The Crow or Raven)

Apollo made love to the princess Coronis. While pregnant with the god's son she lay with a young man called Ischys. She came with her father, King Phlegyas, to the festival at Epidaurus where in her shame she exposed the baby on Mount Myrtium. A goatherd discovered the boy, whose name was Asclepius, being suckled by his goats, but he fled when he saw lightning flashing around him. A white crow had seen Coronis with her mortal lover and it flew to tell Apollo; the god turned it from white to black

and placed it in the night sky as a warning to those who would tell on others. Coronis was shot dead with the arrows of Artemis and Apollo, but her child Asclepius was taught medicine by the centaur Cheiron and became the god of healing; his main cult centre was at Epidaurus.

Crater (The Cup or Bowl)

An alternative story involving the crow of Apollo links the constellation to its neighbours, the Cup (which also has other stories) and the Serpent (usually seen as the Hydra). The crow had been sent to fetch a cup of water from a spring for Apollo. Beside the spring was a fig-tree covered with unripe fruit. The hungry crow delayed its return to Apollo in order to wait for the fruit to ripen. Apollo punished its delay by preventing it from drinking water during the season when figs are ripening. It was placed among the stars with the snake at its feet to stop it drinking the water in the bowl by its head.

118

Cygnus (The Swan)

King Tyndareus of Sparta married Leda; they had a number of famous children including Clytemnestra and Castor; but two of Leda's children, Helen and Polydeuces, had a divine father. Zeus was attracted to Leda and visited her as a swan; she laid an egg and Helen (of Troy) was hatched from it. Zeus reminded men of Helen's miraculous birth by placing the swan high up in the night sky.

Delphinus (The Dolphin)

The dolphin was such a revered creature in ancient Greece that its constellation has been attributed to various myths: the dolphin that swam the seas to find and persuade Amphitrite to marry Poseidon; or a symbol of the Etruscan pirates turned into dolphins by Dionysus when they jumped overboard in fear of the god.

Draco (The Serpent or Dragon)

There are many serpents, both of land and sea, in Greek mythology, and this constellation has been interpreted as a snake thrown at Athene during the battle with the giants; she caught it and threw it into the sky. It was also thought to be Ladon, the serpent who guarded the golden apples tended by the Hesperides for Hera.

Eridanus

Eridanus is a long meandering line of stars whose source is close to Orion the Hunter and which flows down to the horizon. Eridanus was a son of Tethys and Oceanus, and into his waters plunged Phaethon, struck by a thunderbolt hurled by Zeus to put an end to his destructive course across the sky in his father Helius's sun-chariot; on the way he managed to scorch a line across the sky (the Milky Way) and blacken the skin of those who live near the equator. Phaethon's sisters wept for him beside the river Eridanus and were turned into poplar trees which henceforth wept tears of amber. Ancient writers disagree as to which European river was Eridanus, but presumably it was one famous for its deposits of amber.

LEFT *Tintoretto (c1518–94), The Origin of the Milky Way. This version of the myth relates that Hera was tricked into nursing Heracles; upon discovering her mistake she had him snatched away, causing her milk to sprinkle across the heavens. The peacocks are her sacred bird; Zeus' eagle carries his thunderbolts.*

Gemini (The Twins)

Several pairs of men were thought to be represented by Gemini, but most agree that they are the Dioscuri, Castor and Polydeuces (or Pollux). They were the sons of King Tyndareus of Sparta and Leda and had two famous sisters: Clytemnestra (later wife of King Agamemnon) and Helen (of Troy). Their title 'Dioscuri' means 'sons of Zeus', though Castor and Clytemnestra were mortal children of Tyndareus whilst Helen and Polydeuces were fathered by Zeus. The two brothers performed many heroic exploits, their early adventures occurring on the voyage of the Argonauts, where Castor proved himself as a skilled tamer of horses and Polydeuces as a formidable boxer. Later they saved their sister Helen after her abduction to Athens by Theseus, who desired a daughter of Zeus for his wife. There seems to have been a general dearth of marriageable princesses in mythical times and the Dioscuri also went in search of wives, eventually settling on the two beautiful daughters of their uncle Leucippus, Phoebe and Hilaeira; they had to be taken by force as they were already betrothed to their cousins Lynceus and Idas. A fight ensued between the four cousins and when Castor was killed, Polydeuces prayed to his father Zeus that he might share his immortality with his beloved brother: thus they spent alternate days up on Mount Olympus and down in Hades. They were also placed as stars in the sky, forming the twin constellation Gemini, with its two bright stars, Castor and Pollux. They also guarded those in storms at sea, often appearing as balls of fire (later called St Elmo's fire) in the sky: one such ball was a bad omen, representing their sister Helen of Troy, but two balls together was a good sign, representing the twin heroes.

Leo (The Lion)

Placed in the sky by Hera to commemorate the Nemean Lion which fought Heracles without success.

Lepus (The Hare)

Hermes honoured the hare as a constellation for being a swift runner like himself. It appears beneath Orion the Hunter, who is more likely to be chasing Taurus the Bull as a more fitting adversary. The hare was considered an endearing creature and was often given as a love-gift; the people of the island of Leros imported some, but they bred rapidly and began to eat the crops threatening famine; the islanders marched in a line across the island driving the hares into the sea. Some say that the constellation was placed by Artemis as protector of animals.

Libra (The Scales)

Possibly the scales held by Dike, goddess of justice, if she is represented by nearby Virgo.

卐卐卐卐卐卐卐卐卐

BELOW *Peter Paul Rubens (1577–1640),* Rape of the Daughters of Leucippus. *The Dioscuri, Castor and Polydeuces, appear with their two horses; Eros is present and invites the viewer to witness the abduction of the two 'Rubenesque' women.*

Lyra (The Lyre)

Orpheus was the son of the leader of the Muses, Calliope, and Apollo, and he inherited his father's skill with the lyre. In fact, Orpheus played his lyre so beautifully that the whole of nature was enchanted: even trees and rocks would gather around him while he played. He married a Dryad called Eurydice. One day, Aristaeus, another son of Apollo, was chasing Eurydice through the Thracian meadows, when the nymph trod on a snake which bit and poisoned her. Orpheus' sorrow was so great that he determined to rescue her from Hades. Cerberus and Charon allowed him to pass, lulled by his music, and Hades and Persephone were so moved by his lament that they allowed him to depart with Eurydice on the condition that he resisted the temptation to turn around and look at her until they reached Earth. As they approached the light of day, Eurydice refused to go further unless her husband looked at her; Orpheus could not refuse, and turning, saw her fade back into the mists of Hades. Orpheus was not allowed a second chance, and spent the rest of his earthly life in mourning for his doubly lost love.

One story says that Orpheus offended Dionysus because of his adherence to his father, the musical god Apollo, seen by the Greeks as a rational and intellectual deity in comparison to the irrationality and instinct embodied in Dionysus. Dionysus' Maenads tore him to bits, but the Muses gathered up his limbs and buried them in Pieria. They could not find his head or lyre, however, which floated down the river and across the Aegean Sea to the island of Lesbos, where the Lesbians were rewarded with the gift of song for giving his last remains a proper burial. The Muses carried his lyre into the night sky to become the constellation Lyra.

BELOW *Giovanni Bellini (c1430–1516), Orpheus. Representations of Orpheus, the bringer of music to mankind, always portray him with a contemporary stringed instrument: Bellini replaces the Greek lyre with an Italian viol while animals, nymphs and satyrs gather round – even a tree (right) has bent over to listen.*

Ophiuchus (The Serpent-Holder)

Many heroes fought serpents and this constellation therefore has many attributions, but most say that it represents Asclepius, son of Apollo and god of healing; he is often represented holding a snake, associated with his healing powers.

Orion (The Hunter)

In the night sky, the huge constellation of Orion is surrounded by animals; his hunting dog Canis Major runs ahead of him, the hare Lepus scampers away as does Taurus the Bull; some say that he is in endless lusty pursuit of Pleione's seven daughters, whom Zeus immortalized as the star-cluster Pleiades; it is a sign of good eyesight to be able to count all seven stars. Orion was the son of Euryale, daughter of Minos of Crete, and Poseidon. His father gave him the ability to walk over the sea and his adventures took him from island to island.

RIGHT The Gorgon Medusa; *sculpted pediment from the temple of Artemis at Corfu, early 6th century* BC. *Gorgons were often used on religious buildings to frighten away evil spirits. The kneeling pose was used by Archaic artists to denote running. Her children appear on each side in front of the leopards: Pegasus is damaged but his back legs are visible (left); Chrysaor appears (right). Fighting groups, probably from the Trojan legends, fill the corners. The frontal images and fractured composition are typical of early Archaic art.*

On Chios, Orion was invited by King Oenopion to hunt and destroy all the wild animals of the island; in return, Oenopion promised his daughter Merope in marriage to the giant. Orion cleared the island in a day and at the celebratory banquet demanded his prize; Oenopion denied all knowledge of the offer and plied his heroic guest with wine. That night the drunken Orion raped Merope and Oenopion had him blinded in revenge, dumping his body on the beach. Orion walked the waves across to

Lemnos where Hephaestus worked a forge; Orion caught hold of Celadion, one of the divine blacksmith's apprentices, and made him stand on his shoulders to guide his way. The giant was lead eastwards and the light of Helius cured his blindness; he returned to Chios to kill Oenopion, but angry Hephaestus had hidden the king underground. Celadion was returned to Lemnos and Orion settled on Crete, where he hunted with Artemis.

Artemis' brother Apollo became jealous of the giant. One day when Orion was wading off the coast with only his head above the waves, Apollo pointed out what appeared to be a piece of driftwood to Artemis and gave her first shot at it as target practice. The arrow found its mark and the goddess set Orion among the stars. Some say, however, that he threatened to hunt down all the animals in the world; Gaia sent a scorpion to kill him and Zeus placed him in the night sky alongside the scorpion (Scorpio) at the request of Artemis.

Pegasus (The Winged Horse)

Pegasus was born from the neck of the Gorgon Medusa when Perseus cut her head off. His father was Poseidon, god of horses. Pegasus was tamed by the hero Bellerophon who killed many foes with the help of his magical steed, but when he tried to reach the heights of Olympus, Zeus sent a gadfly to sting the horse which reared up to dislodge his rider; Bellerophon fell to his death whilst Pegasus continued on to Olympus to become the bearer of Zeus' thunder-

bolts. Zeus honoured Pegasus with a constellation, depicting him on his way to heaven.

Perseus

The hero took his place among the stars standing above Cetus the sea-monster whom he slew to win the hand of Andromeda, who stands beside him.

Pisces (The Fish)

After the battle of the gods and Titans, Gaia gave birth to the monster Typhon as a last attempt to conquer the gods. Although Zeus eventually defeated him, the other gods turned and ran. Typhon encountered Eros and Aphrodite on the banks of the river Euphrates; they turned themselves into fish, leaping into the river to escape. These two gods thus appear as a pair of fish in the sky.

Pleiades (The Seven Daughters of Pleione and Atlas)

Merope alone took a mortal husband, and her star is therefore the dimmest of the seven. Her sisters had famous children by Zeus, Poseidon, Hermes and Ares; Zeus turned them into stars to escape the lustful approaches of the hunter Orion, but he too became a constellation and still pursues them across the night sky.

Scorpio (The Scorpion)

Although it appears on the other side of the sky from Orion, the constellation represents the huge scorpion sent as a punishment by Gaia to kill the giant hunter for his threat to destroy all the world's animals.

Taurus (The Bull)

Zeus used the form of a handsome white bull on two amorous occasions: to make love to Io when she was in the form of a cow; and to abduct the princess Europa of Tyre when she was playing with her friends on the beach. Europa showed no interest in him until he lay down to chew a crocus; thinking him unusually sweet and gentle for a bull, she sat on his back but the laughter of her companions soon turned to screams as the bull swam out to sea with his new lover. They arrived at Crete and Europa had several children by the god including Minos; the bull and its horns remained important elements in Cretan art, myth and ritual. The bull was placed in the sky above Orion whom some say pursues it rather than the less noble hare.

Ursa Major and Ursa Minor (The Great and Little Bears)

The Great Bear was actually called Arctos (Bear) by the Greeks, Ursa Major being its Roman name. Zeus made love to Callisto, the Arcadian nymph and friend of Artemis, who was turned into a bear by Hera in her jealous anger. Callisto's son by Zeus was Arcas, who grew up in the woods where he one day shot his own mother, thinking her to be a wild boar. Zeus immortalized mother and son as constellations: Arcas became Arctophylax (The Bear-Keeper or Herdsman) who appears to watch over Ursa Major. Hera's anger increased at this celebration of Zeus' infidelity; she asked Tethys, her former nurse, and Oceanus never to allow the Great Bear to enter their waters, as the other constellations do when they set. Ursa Major was therefore doomed to wander together with Ursa Minor eternally around Polaris (the north star) and remains ever visible in the night sky.

Virgo (The Virgin)

Ancient writers disagree as to who is represented by this constellation; candidates include Dike (Justice) who might then be holding the scales of the neighbouring constellation Libra. Curiously the goddess Demeter is another suggestion, even though she had several children.

LEFT The Rape of Europa; *Roman wall-painting from a Pompeian house, 1st century AD. The pyramidal composition suggests that this copies a lost Late Classical Greek easel-painting. The princess is posed gracefully and no one seems aware of the bull's real identity except the bull himself, who looks out knowingly at the viewer.*

Appendix

SOURCES

The following ancient authors dealt with mythological subjects and can be readily obtained in translation in paperback editions:

GREEK AUTHORS
The tragedies of Aeschylus, Euripides and Sophocles
Herodotus, *The Persian Wars*
The poems of Hesiod, Homer, Pindar, Sappho, Theocritus
Pausanias, *Description of Greece*
Plutarch, *Parallel Lives*
The philosophical dialogues of Plato

ROMAN AUTHORS
The poems of Catallus, Horace, Lucretius, Propertius, Vergil and Ovid (especially his 'Metamorphoses' and 'Heroides')
Apuleius, *The Golden Ass*

FURTHER READING

The following modern studies of Greek Mythology are also of interest:

Bremmer, J (ed)
Interpretations of Greek Mythology
(London, 1987)

Dodds, E R
The Greeks and the Irrational
(Berkeley, 1968)

Henle, Jane
Greek Myths: A Vase Painter's Notebook
(Bloomington, 1973)

Kerenyi, C
The Gods of the Greeks
(London, 1974)

Kerenyi, C
The Heroes of the Greeks
(London, 1974)

Kirk, G S
The Nature of Greek Myths
(Baltimore, 1974)

Lefkowitz, M
Women in Greek Myth
(London, 1986)

Schefold, K
Myth and Legend in Early Greek Art
(New York, 1966)

Seznec, J
The Survival of the Pagan Gods; The Mythological Tradition and its Place in Renaissance Humanism and Art
(Guildford, 1961)

A NOTE ON GREEK
AND ROMAN SPELLING

The Romanized spellings of Greek names have been used throughout, since they are the ones that generally occur in modern (post-Renaissance) literature and art. Moreover, many painters and writers have tended to adopt the Roman equivalent names of Greek gods and heroes. Below is a list of the more familiar Greek mythical figures together with their Roman spellings, Greek spelling where it differs and Roman equivalent names where they arise. Note that the Greek '-os' endings often become '-us' in their Romanized Latin forms and that, properly speaking, the 'c' in the Greek names (but not 'ch') should become a 'k' (for example, Achilleus, Narkissos, Kirke); likewise the Greek '-ai-' becomes Roman '-ae-'. Names that do not change have been omitted (for example, Echo, Prometheus, Theseus, Perseus).

ROMAN SPELLING	GREEK SPELLING	ROMAN EQUIVALENT
Achilles	Achilleus	—
Actaeon	Aktaion	—
Ajax	Aias	—
APHRODITE	—	VENUS
APOLLO	APOLLON	—
ARES	—	MARS
ARTEMIS	—	DIANA
Asclepius	Asklepios	Aesculapius
ATHENE (Athena)	—	MINERVA
Cephalus	Kephalos	—
Cerberus	Kerberos	—
Coeus	Koios	—
Crius	Krios	—
Cronus	Kronos	Saturn
Daedalus	Daidalos	—
DEMETER	—	CERES
DIONYSUS	DIONYSOS	BACCHUS
Eos	—	Aurora
Erebus	Erebos	—
Erinyes	—	Furies
Eros	—	Cupid (or Amor)
Gaea (or Ge)	Gaia (or Ge)	Tellus (or Terra)
Graeae	Graiai	—
HADES	HAIDES	PLUTO (or Dis)
Hebe	—	Juventas (or Juventus)
Helius	Helios	Sol
Hemera	—	Dies
HEPHAESTUS	HEPHAISTOS	VULCAN
HERA (or Here)	—	JUNO
Heracles	Herakles	Hercules
HERMES	—	MERCURY
HESTIA	—	VESTA
Iapetus	Iapetos	—
Icarus	Ikaros	—
Jocasta	Iokaste	—
Moerae	Moirai	Fates
Narcissus	Narkissos	—
Nike	—	Victory
Nyx	—	Nox
Oceanus	Okeanos	—
Oedipus	Oidipous	—
Olympus	Olympos	—
Persephone	—	Proserpina
Plutus	Ploutos	—
POSEIDON	—	NEPTUNE
Pyramus	Pyramos	—
Rhea	—	Ops
Seirenes	—	Sirens
Selene	—	Luna
Tartarus	Tartaros	—
Tyche	—	Fortune
Uranus	Ouranos	Caelus
ZEUS	—	JUPITER

Index

Acknowledgements

KEY: *t* = top; *b* = bottom; *l* = left; *r* = right; *c* = centre.

Acropolis Museum, Athens: PAGES 27, 32 ● American School of Classical Studies at Athens – Agora Excavations: PAGES 8 *l*, 30/31 ● Ashmolean Museum, Oxford: PAGES 7 *r*, 8 *tr cr*, 21, 87, 94 *b* ● Photo David Bellingham: PAGES 6, 7 *l*, 8 *br*, 35 *b*, 37, 38, 42, 44 *r*, 48/49, 50, 68, 69 *t b*, 7 *l*, 88/89, 102, 109, 117 ● Reproduced by permission of the Birmingham Museum and Art Gallery: PAGE 40 ● Bridgeman Art Library: PAGES 10/11 (Uffizi Gallery, Florence); 78/79 (Alte Pinakothek, Munich); 101 (Manchester City Art Gallery); 111 (Musée des Beaux-Arts, Bruxelles); 120 (Alte Pinakothek, Munich) ● Reproduced by courtesy of the Trustees of the British Museum, London: front jacket, rear endpapers and PAGES 13, 31, 43, 54, 56, 66/67, 72, 76, 77 *b*, 80, 84/85, 86, 93 *t*, 98, 98/99 ● Photo Pauline Cole: PAGE 64 ● Corfu Museum: PAGE 122 ● Delphi Museum: PAGE 26 *b* ● Eleusis Museum: PAGE 91 ● Photo Christine Grande: PAGE 28 *t* ● Musée du Louvre: PAGES 34, 35 *t*, 44 *l*, 60/61, 62, 63, 75, 81, 95 ● Museo Archeologico Regionale di Palermo, Sicily: PAGES 17 *t*, 52/53, 84 ● Museo Archeologico Regionale 'P. Orsi', Siracusa: PAGE 12 ● Museo Nationale, Naples: PAGES 16, 77 *t*, 122/123 ● Copyright © Museo del Prado, Madrid: PAGES 14/15, 20, 23, 24, 38/39, 82/83, 108 ● Collection, Museum of Modern Art, New York: PAGE 65 ● National Archeological Museum, Athens: PAGES 25, 28 *b*, 41, 60 ● Reproduced by courtesy of the Trustees, The National Gallery, London: PAGES 19, 46/47, 92, 96/97, 99, 106/107, 110, 112, 118, 119 ● National Gallery of Art, Washington: PAGES 36 (Andrew W. Mellon Collection); 79 (Chester Dale Collection); 93 *b* (Samuel H. Kress Collection); 100 (Widener Collection); 104 (Widener Collection); 105 (Samuel H. Kress Collection); 113 (Samuel H. Kress Collection); 121 (Widener Collection) ● National Museum, Department of Near Eastern and Classical Archeology, Copenhagen: PAGE 33 (100801) ● Olympia Museum: PAGES 39 *t*, 55, 61, 116 ● Pergamon Museum, Berlin: PAGE 22 ● Piraeus Museum: PAGE 26 *t* ● Rijksmuseum van Oudheden, Leiden: PAGES 45, 51 ● Royal Ontario Museum, Toronto: back jacket and PAGE 29 ● Photo Robert Simons: PAGE 70 *t b* ● Southampton City Art Gallery, UK: PAGE 85 ● Photo Vatican Museums: PAGES 58, 94 *t* ● Visual Arts Library: PAGES 11 (Art Institute of Chicago); 17 *b* (Boston Museum of Fine Arts); 18 (Musée des Beaux-Arts, Bruxelles); 107 (The National Gallery, London), 115 (Uffizi Gallery, Florence) ● Walker Art Gallery, Liverpool: PAGE 103.